SAT ATTA

Badger KS3 Maths Tes uides

Supplies of Ammunition to help make your Maths Exam Mission Possible

Book 1 ~ for levels 3-6

David Kent, Joan Knott,
Colin Murray, Liz Rimmer

Badger Publishing

Introduction

This book has been written to help you to prepare for your National Curriculum Key Stage 3 tests in Mathematics.

The material required for the tests both with and without a calculator at

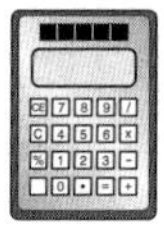

Levels 3 ~ 5
and
Levels 4 ~ 6

are covered in this book.

Your teacher is likely to give you some tests before you do the real one. These tests should help to give you confidence, particularly as you will find which areas of mathematics you are already good at. Don't panic ~ the questions you got wrong will provide an opportunity for you to improve your skills and gain marks.

Every skill you master can help you gain another mark (or more) when you do the real thing. The questions in this book should help you to develop the skills you need. You should use the questions to help improve the skills already established and use the explanations to help you understand the areas in which you require help. Talking it through with friends, relatives, parents or your teacher can always help.

Each National Curriculum test has a **total** of **sixty** marks. So in test **3-5** and test **4-6** there are likely to be:

Test 3-5		**Test 4-6**	
Level 3	20 marks		
Level 4	20 marks	Level 4	20 marks
Level 5	20 marks	Level 5	20 marks
		Level 6	20 marks

In the Teacher Book, there are a range of test questions that your teacher can put together to give you an idea of what grade you are likely to receive for your real test. We would suggest that, by putting these tests together, you should get a fairly good idea of whether it is best for you to take **Test 3-5** or **Test 4-6** when you take the NC tests. This table might provide you with some advice:

Test mark	**Test suggested**	**Alternative test**
Less than 30	3-5	None
30-50	3-5	4-6
51-60	4-6	At least 4-6

Please remember that the very best way of revising mathematics is to do some questions and in the material of this book we have prepared many questions which will help you with your revision.

We hope that you enjoy working from this book and that by doing so you can improve your level in the Key Stage 3 test.

David Kent, Joan Knott, Colin Murray, Liz Rimmer

Advice on taking the tests

Each question in a test will inform you of how many marks a correct answer is worth.

Many questions are worth **1 mark**, so it is really a question of your answer being **right** to obtain that mark. Here is an example of one, taken from the paper set on levels 3-5 in the summer of 2003.

Look at this diagram.
It shows the distance in miles between some cities.

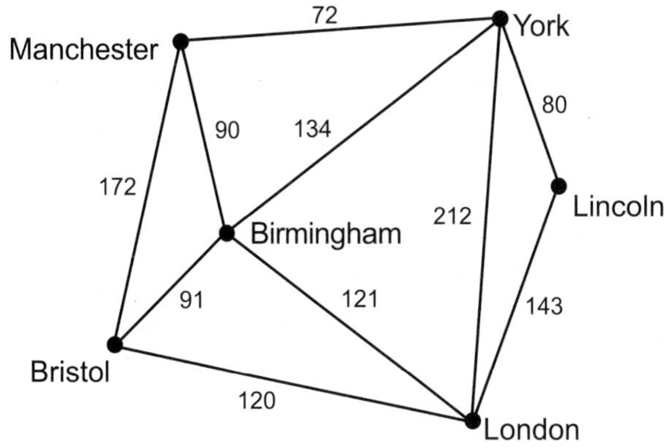

a) How far is it from Bristol to Manchester?

. . . . miles. *1 mark*

All you need to do, with this question, is read off the distance **172** from the map and write it down as your answer.

However some questions are worth more than 1 mark, perhaps even more than **2 marks**. Here is an example from the same topic as the previous question set in 2003, it is part (d).

d) Sanjay drives from **London to Bristol**, then he drives to **Birmingham**, and then he drives directly back **to London**.

How many miles does he drive altogether?
Show your working.

. . . . miles. *2 marks*

If you just write the answer down as **332** miles without showing your working then, providing your answer is correct, you are likely to only be awarded 1 mark. You have been asked to **show your working** and you have not done so. The correct answer, with working, is:

120 + 91 + 121 = 332 miles

The likelihood is that you will get **1** mark for showing 120 + 91 + 121, and **1 mark** for the correct answer.

Make sure you are in a position to get all the marks that you can.

Revising for the tests

Mathematics should be revised actively, not merely by reading nor by writing answers down.

We now offer you a list of things to do with your revision:

- It is usually best to revise in short burst of about half an hour, with a break afterwards.
- It is often best to revise in a small group of two or three people.
- Summarise the main facts, results and formulae.
- Write down any key facts or formulae that you have learnt.
- Practice reading facts and formulae out loud, preferably to a friend.
- Work through any sources of examples you can find, especially those given in this text and by your teacher.
- Try some examples and check your solutions.
- Try some questions from previous papers.
- Highlight any key words that you are often asked about in questions.
- Look at the different types of questions such as:
  - Those that ask you to CALCULATE;
  - Those that ask you to EXPLAIN and;
  - Those that ask you to SHOW;

  and be sure that you 'Do what you are asked to do'.
- Make notes about anything you do not understand and ask questions about it to your teacher or a friend.
- Make absolutely sure that you turn up for the examination at the right time.

And the very best of luck to you and everybody else.

Contents

Please note all levels are approximate.

Basic number work 1

Mental recall

You will almost certainly be asked to add or subtract two numbers both of which are no bigger than **20**.

Can you work out **17 – 4** in your head?

Whole numbers like 17 are called **integers.**

This could easily be a question which appears in your **mental arithmetic test**.

In the mental test the numbers, like **17** and **4**, will be read out as **seventeen** and **four**.

Adding and subtracting two and three digit numbers.

There are also questions like: 35 + 27 This is adding two two-digit numbers.
or 581 – 325 This is subtracting two three-digit numbers.

with these responses:

$$\begin{array}{r} 35\ + \\ \underline{27} \\ 62 \end{array} \qquad \begin{array}{r} 581\ - \\ \underline{325} \\ 256 \end{array}$$

You will almost certainly be asked to do these questions **without using a calculator**, and there may even be some simple ones in the **mental arithmetic test**.

Making approximations

683 *is* 680 when it is rounded to the nearest ten because **3** is less than 5.

683 *is* 700 when it is rounded to the nearest hundred because **83** is greater then 50.

We round down for the numbers **0**, **1**, **2**, **3** and **4**.

173 rounds down to become **170** to the nearest 10,

but **173** rounds *up* to become **200** to the nearest 100.

We **round up** for the numbers **5**, **6**, **7**, **8** and **9**.

Decimals and negative numbers

Money is an example where numbers use **decimals**.

£3.74 means 3 pounds and 74 pence.

-2	-1	0	1	2	3	4

0 is the ground floor.

You can see signs like this in lifts. It means that the lift goes from **2 floors below the ground** to **4 floors above the ground**.

Basic number work 1 ~ Questions

1. **Write down the answers to:**

a) 16 + 8 b) 14 – 5 c) 17 + 6
d) 17 – 8 e) 21 + 9 f) 32 – 18
g) 15 – 6 h) 38 – 5 i) 43 + 57
j) 26 – 17 k) 75 – 16 l) 26 – 19

2. **Work out:**

a) 45 + 37 b) 48 – 12 c) 53 + 11
d) 520 – 20 e) 632 – 32 f) 632 – 35
g) 482 – 212 h) 584 – 327 i) 481 + 325
j) 700 – 7 k) 742 + 137 l) 531 – 257
m) 825 – 196 n) 498 + 203 o) 430 + 278

3. **Round these numbers:**

a) 582 to the nearest 10
b) 473 to the nearest 100
c) 651 to the nearest 100
d) 286 to the nearest 10

4. **Write these in figures:**

a) 4 pounds and 68 pence
b) 3 pounds and 20 pence
c) 17 pounds and 2 pence
d) 24 pounds only
e) 36 pounds and 52 pence
f) ten pounds and thirty pence
g) six pounds and twelve pence
h) one hundred and thirty two pounds
i) seventeen hundred and forty pounds and fifty pence.

5. **The lift shaft in Blackwell's store has a floor sign like this.**

-2	-1	0	1	2	3	4	5

How many floors are there:

a) between -2 and 4

b) between -1 and 2

6. **The depth to the bottom of a lake is 50 metres.**
At the side of the lake there is a cliff.
The height of the cliff is 30 metres.
What is the distance from the bottom of the lake to the top of the cliff?

Basic number work 2

Multiplying and dividing by 10 and 100

Hundreds	Tens	Units	
	3	7	x
	1	0	
3	7	0	

37 x 100 = 3700

Similarly 520 ÷ 10 = 52   1000 ÷ 100 = 10

You could be asked to multiply **any** number by either 10 or 100.
This could be asked in either a written test or a mental test.

Mental computation
Here are some quite simple computations:

3 x 4 + 2 = 12 + 2 = 14   **(multiply before adding)**
(**5 – 1**) x 7 = **4** x 7 = 28   **(always do what is in the brackets first)**
28 – 6 x 4 = 28 – 24 = 4
45 ÷ (5 x 3) = 45 ÷ 15 = 3

These questions can often appear in the mental test.
Remember, the numbers are usually read out aloud, so
3 x 4 + 2 would be read out as 'Multiply three by four and then add two'.

More calculations
Here are some other calculations:

27 + 35 – 12 =   32 x 6 =
48 ÷ 4 =   56 ÷ (6 + 2) =

You should be able to do them all and others like them.
Check that the answers are about right. That is **30 x 6** is about **180**.

Adding, subtracting and ordering decimals

$\frac{3}{10} = 0.3$ $\frac{8}{10} = 0.8$

$\frac{29}{100} = 0.29$ $0.04 = \frac{4}{100} = \frac{2}{50}$

$$\begin{array}{r} 0.37 \\ +\ 0.25 \\ \hline 0.62 \end{array} \qquad \begin{array}{r} 0.37 \\ -\ 0.25 \\ \hline 0.08 \end{array}$$

Basic number work 2 ~ Questions

1. Work out:

a) 42 x 10
b) 5 x 100
c) 17 x 10
d) 10 x 10
e) 26 x 100
f) 68 x 100
g) 100 x 20
h) 34 x 2 x 10
i) 34 x 20
j) 50 ÷ 10
k) 5100 ÷ 100
l) 480 ÷ 10
m) 650 ÷ 10
n) 1600 ÷ 100
o) 2700 ÷ 10

2. Work out each result:

a) 4 x 7 – 3 = ___
b) 5 x 6 – 7 = ___
c) 18 ÷ 3 + 4 = ___
d) 27 ÷ 9 – 2 = ___

3. Work out the missing number:

a) 3 x □ – 1 = 14
b) (16 ÷ □) + 2 = 6
c) □ x 2 – 7 = 3
d) □ ÷ 5 + 2 = 12

4. Write each of these as they could appear in a mental test:

a) (20 ÷ 5) + 1 =
b) (16 + 2) ÷ 3 =
c) (50 ÷ 10) – 4 =
d) (24 ÷ 4) + 3 =
e) 5 x 6 + 3 =
f) (15 – 6) x 4 =
g) (4 + 3) x 5 – 1 =
h) (18 + 12 – 10) ÷ 5 =

5. Check to see which answers are reasonable:

a) 31 x 6 = 186
b) 400 ÷ 8 = 50
c) 300 ÷ 5 = 6
d) (1400 + 200) ÷ 2 = 80
e) 120 x 5 = 600
f) 600 ÷ 6 = 10

6. Work out:

a) 0.3 + 0.4
b) 0.23 + 0.18
c) 0.57 – 0.14
d) 0.43 – 0.17
e) 1.23 + 1.67
f) 2.13 – 1.09

7. Write these sequences of numbers in order:

Start each time with the smallest.

a) 0.25, 0.17, 0.07, 0.22
b) 0.01, 0.2, 0.3, 0.17
c) 0.5, 0.3, 0.6, 0.2
d) 0.61, 0.60, 6.1, 1.6
e) 0.47, 0.41, 0.04, 4.1

Basic multiplication and division

You need to know **all** your **multiplication** facts from 1 x 1 to 10 x 10.

Here are the results ~ set out in a table: you need to know **all** the results.

x	1	2	3	4	5	6	7	8	9	10
1	1	2	3	4	5	6	7	8	9	10
2	2	4	6	8	10	12	14	16	18	20
3	3	6	9	12	15	18	21	24	27	30
4	4	8	12	16	20	24	**28**	32	36	40
5	5	10	15	20	25	30	35	40	45	50
6	6	12	18	24	30	36	42	48	54	60
7	7	14	21	28	35	42	49	56	63	70
8	8	16	24	32	40	48	56	64	72	80
9	9	18	27	36	**45**	54	63	72	81	90
10	10	20	30	40	50	60	70	80	90	100

This means that 4 x 7 = 28.

This means that 9 x 5 = 45.

The table tells you that **4 x 7 = 28**

and that **9 x 5 = 45.**

You are also expected to know the **division** facts associated with this table.

In the table we have **4 x 7 = 28.**

4 and 7 are **factors** of 28.

So we can say that **28 ÷ 4 = 7** or **28 ÷ 7 = 4.**

Sometimes, when you do a **division sum** there will be a **remainder**.

Here is one with a remainder:

53 ÷ 8 = 6 remainder 5

8 x 6 = 48, 48 is 5 less than 53

So this **5** is the **remainder**.

Number 1

Basic multiplication and division ~ Questions

1. Try to do these questions without using the table:

a) 2 x 3 = b) 2 x 5 = c) 2 x 6 = d) 2 x 9 = e) 2 x 4 =

f) 3 x 4 = g) 3 x 7 = h) 3 x 9 = i) 3 x 10 = j) 3 x 3 =

k) 4 x 4 = l) 4 x 5 = m) 4 x 7 = n) 4 x 9 = o) 4 x 3 =

p) 5 x 2 = q) 5 x 8 = r) 5 x 4 = s) 5 x 10 = t) 5 x 5 =

u) 10 x 10 = v) 10 x 3 = w) 10 x 7 = x) 10 x 9 = y) 10 x 6 =

2. Using the table of values, find:

a) 6 x 4 = b) 7 x 9 = c) 8 x 3 = d) 8 x 6 = e) 6 x 9 =

f) 9 x 3 = g) 8 x 7 = h) 9 x 9 = i) 9 x 8 = j) 7 x 6 =

k) 6 x 6 = l) 7 x 7 = m) 8 x 4 = n) 8 x 9 = o) 9 x 8 =

3. Copy and complete, placing the missing numbers in the boxes.

a) 3 x □ = 15 b) 2 x □ = 10 c) □ x 4 = 20 d) □ x 3 = 12

e) 5 x □ = 25 f) 7 x □ = 42 g) □ x 6 = 48 h) □ x 9 = 54

i) □ x □ = 15 j) □ x □ = 24 k) □ x □ = 32 l) □ x □ = 30

m) □ x □ = 56 n) □ x □ = 100 o) □ x □ = 0 p) □ x □ = 63

4. Use the table of values to help you to work out the answers.

a) 6 ÷ 2 = b) 21 ÷ 3 = c) 16 ÷ 4 = d) 24 ÷ 3 = e) 10 ÷ 5 =

f) 18 ÷ 2 = g) 30 ÷ 3 = h) 40 ÷ 5 = i) 28 ÷ 4 = j) 48 ÷ 4 =

k) 54 ÷ 6 = l) 100 ÷ 10 = m) 24 ÷ 8 = n) 63 ÷ 7 = o) 72 ÷ 9 =

p) 36 ÷ 9 = q) 56 ÷ 8 = r) 49 ÷ 7 = s) 48 ÷ 8 = t) 35 ÷ 7 =

5. These questions have remainders.
Use the table of values to help you to work out the answers.

a) 16 ÷ 3 = b) 22 ÷ 3 = c) 47 ÷ 5 = d) 70 ÷ 8 =

e) 25 ÷ 8 = f) 52 ÷ 7 = g) 62 ÷ 6 = h) 75 ÷ 9 =

Multiplication

Multiplying by 10

5 x 10 = 50

15 x 10 = 150

215 x 10 = 2150

Multiplying by 20, 30... 200, 300

5 x 30 = 5 x 10 x 3 = 50 x 3 = 150

23 x 30 = 23 x 10 x 3 = 230 x 3

Multiplying by 30 Is the same as multiplying by 10 then by 3.

```
 230
x  3
 690
```

15 x 500 = 15 x 100 x 5

= 1500 x 5

```
 1500
x   5
 7500
```

Long multiplication

231 x 45

Break the sum down: 45 = 40 + 5

231 x 40 = 9240

231 x 5 = 1155

Add = 10,395

Multiplication ~ Questions

The first SAT paper does not allow you to use a calculator. It is useful to keep one handy whilst you are practising so that you can check your answers.

1. a) 215 x 10 b) 342 x 100

c) 32 x 1000 d) 247 x 1000

2. a) 215 x 20 b) 342 x 300

c) 32 x 6000 d) 247 x 7000

3. a) 235 x 17 b) 142 x 23

c) 32 x 67 d) 257 x 85

e) 115 x 24 f) 347 x 37

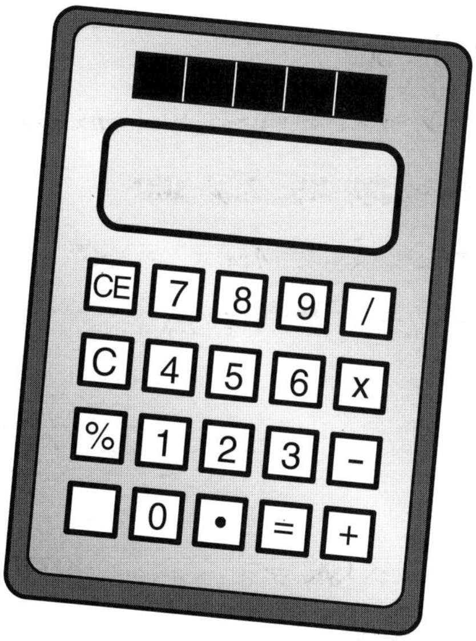

4. Colin can type 27 words per minute on his computer keyboard.
How many words can he type in 30 minutes?

5. Ann is training for the 100m.
She completes the distance 27 times during a training session.
How far has she run in training?

6. 47 students each made 24 cakes to sell on a cake stall.
How many cakes did they have for sale?

7. A school bought 36 bags of counters.
Each bag contains 144 counters.
How many counters did the school have altogether?

8. Jo is trying to get fit!
He decides to do 25 press-ups every day.
How many will he complete in a year (365 days)?

Division

Dividing by 10

1000 ÷ 10 = 100
1200 ÷ 10 = 120
1230 ÷ 10 = 123
1234 ÷ 10 = 123.4

1000 ÷ 100 = 10
1200 ÷ 100 = 12
300,000 ÷ 10 = 30,000

1000 ÷ 20 = (1000 ÷ 10) ÷ 2
= 100 ÷ 2
= 50

1200 ÷ 60 = (1200 ÷ 10) ÷ 6
= 120 ÷ 6
= 20

Long division

Work out an estimate first.

Example: 786 ÷ 23
786 is almost 800.
23 is a bit more than 20.
800 ÷ 20 is (800 ÷ 10) ÷ 2
= 80 ÷ 2 = 40

Try 23 x 40 = 23 x 10 x 4
230 x 4 = 920 ~ too big!!!

Next try 23 x 30 = 23 x 10 x 3
230 x 3 = 690

786 – 690 = 96

So 23 divides into 786 30 times with 96 left over.

> Our answer lies between 30 and 40.

We need 96 ÷ 23 =
Again estimate 96 is almost 100.
23 is just more than 20.

100 ÷ 20 = 5
23 x 5 = 115 ~ too big!!!

So try 23 x 4 = 92

> The answer must be just less than 35. Lets try 4.

786 = 30 x 23 = 690
+ 4 x 23 = 92
34 x 23 = 782

786 ÷ 23 = 34 remainder 4

Division ~ Questions

1. a) $200 \div 10$ b) $300 \div 100$

   c) $30{,}000 \div 1000$ d) $2000 \div 100$

2. a) $210 \div 10$ b) $330 \div 100$

   c) $3200 \div 100$ d) $24{,}000 \div 1000$

3. a) $200 \div 40$ b) $300 \div 50$

   c) $3300 \div 300$ d) $2400 \div 60$

4. a) $210 \div 15$ b) $330 \div 22$

   c) $3200 \div 40$ d) $24{,}000 \div 48$

5. **A holiday company has sold 252 seats for a coach trip.**
   If a coach has 54 seats how many coaches will be needed?
   (Everyone must have a seat.)
   How many spare seats will they have?

6. **A school is planning a disco for 844 pupils.**
   They want to provide a can of drink for each pupil.
   The cans came in packs of 24.
   How many packs are needed?

7. **The storage tank of a petrol pump holds 26,000 litres of petrol.**
   How many cars' tanks holding 45 litres of fuel can be filled up from the tank?

8. **A lottery prize of £3,500,000 is shared by 18 people.**
   How much does each person get?

9. **A brick wall contains 7344 bricks.**
   Each row contains 272 bricks.
   How many bricks high was the wall?

Fractions and percentages 1

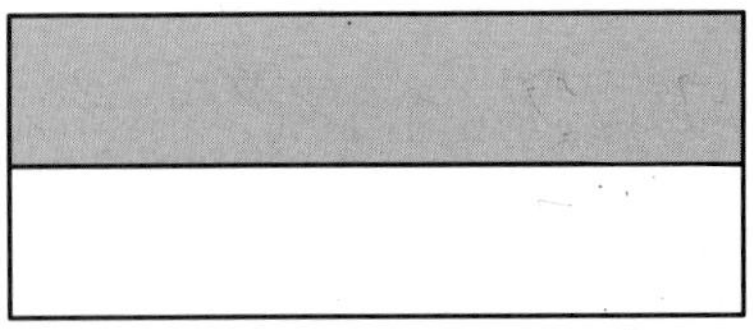

This shaded part is

$$\frac{1}{2}$$

$\{ \frac{1}{2} \rightarrow \frac{\text{the numerator}}{\text{the denominator}} \}$

of the rectangle.

This shaded part is

$$\frac{3}{6}$$

of the rectangle.

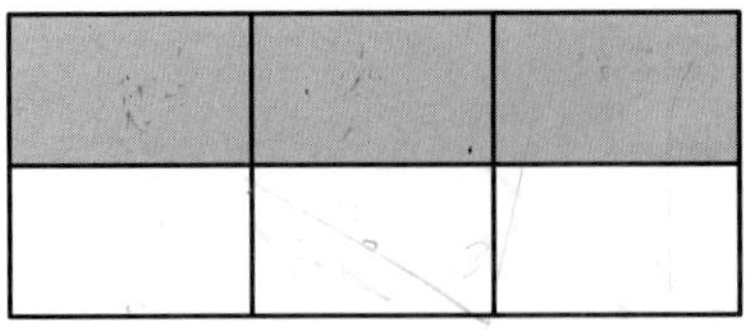

The two fractions $\frac{1}{2}$ and $\frac{3}{6}$ are equivalent.

$$\frac{3}{6} = \frac{3 \times 1}{3 \times 2} = \frac{\cancel{3} \times 1}{\cancel{3} \times 2} = \frac{1}{2}$$

Here are two other equivalent fractions:

$\frac{3}{5}$ and $\frac{9}{15}$ are equivalent.

$$\frac{9}{15} = \frac{\cancel{3} \times 3}{\cancel{3} \times 5} = \frac{3}{5}$$

Here is the fraction $\frac{3}{5}$:

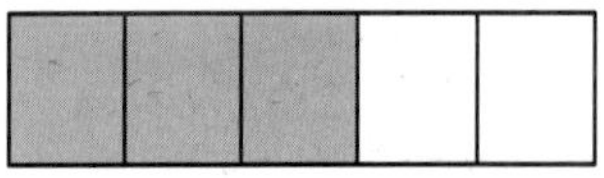

But $\frac{3}{5}$ is equivalent to $\frac{60}{100}$:

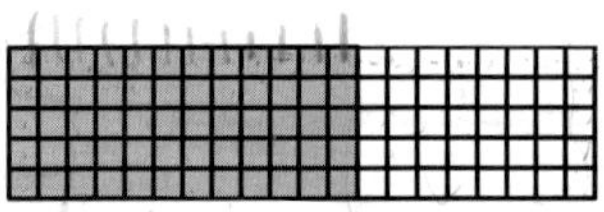

The fraction $\frac{60}{100}$ is often written as 60% ~ 'sixty per cent' ~ or called 60 per cent.

We can work out 40% of 20: XXXXXXXXXX XXXXXXXXXX } 20

$$40\% = \frac{40}{100} = \frac{4}{10} = \frac{2}{5}$$

So 40% of 20 = $\frac{2}{5}$ of 20.

$\frac{1}{5}$ of 20 is [XX XX] so $\frac{2}{5}$ of 20 is [XX XX] [XX XX]

2 boxes = 8. So 40% of 20 = 8.

Fractions and percentages 1 ~ Questions

1. Write down the fraction of each shape that has been shaded.

a) 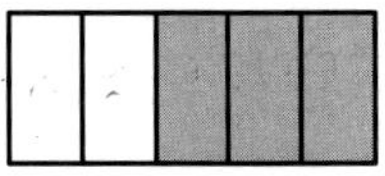 b)  c) 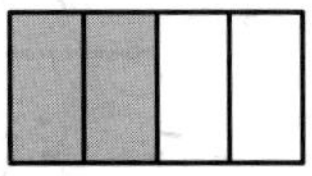

d) 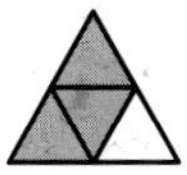 e)  f) 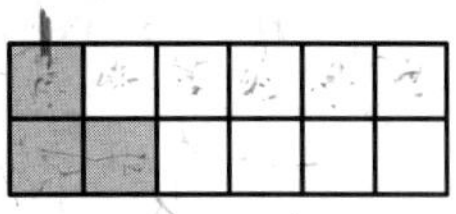

2. Here is the fraction $\frac{3}{4}$:  **Copy and complete:**

a) Show by shading 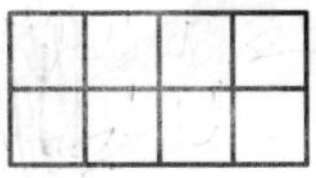, that the fraction $\frac{3}{4}$ is equivalent to $\frac{6}{8}$.

b) Write down any other fraction which is equivalent to $\frac{3}{4}$.

3. Copy and complete each line:

a) $\frac{1}{2} = \frac{}{4} = \frac{3}{} = \frac{4}{} = \frac{}{28}$

b) $\frac{1}{3} = \frac{4}{} = \frac{}{18} = \frac{}{}$

c) $\frac{3}{5} = \frac{}{10} = \frac{12}{} = \frac{}{100} = \quad\%$

4. Copy and complete. Shade 75% of 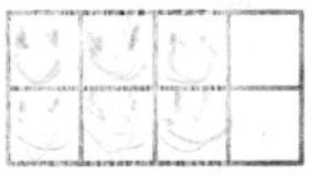

5. Copy and complete. Shade 30% of 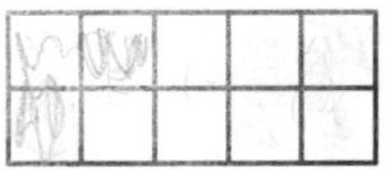

6. Convert each fraction to a percentage.

a) $\frac{1}{2}$ b) $\frac{1}{4}$ c) $\frac{1}{5}$

d) $\frac{2}{5}$ e) $\frac{3}{4}$ f) $\frac{6}{10}$

g) $\frac{13}{20}$ h) $\frac{12}{25}$ i) $\frac{47}{50}$

7. Convert each percentage to a fraction.

a) 30% b) 50% c) 40%

d) 45% e) 20% f) 55%

g) 65% h) 72% i) 80%

Fractions and percentages 2

Fractions

Why does everyone worry about fractions?

A fraction is just a part of something.

The bottom number (**Denominator**) tells us how many parts in the whole.

It is the dividing number or divisor.

The top number (**Numerator**) tells us how many of those parts we have.

It is the multiplying number.

$\frac{3}{4}$ means 3 out of a total of 4 parts.

If I want $\frac{3}{4}$ of something, I find $\frac{1}{4}$ and then find 3 of these.

Example:

Find $\frac{3}{4}$ of £20.

$\frac{1}{4}$ of £20 = £5

$\frac{3}{4}$ of £20 = £15

Percentages

Percent means 'per 100'.

76% means 76 out of every 100 or $\frac{76}{100}$.

Example:

Amy got 80% on her Maths test.

The test was marked out of 120.

How many marks did she get?

1% of 120 is 120/100 = 1.2

Amy achieved 80% = 80 x 1.2 = 96 marks

Find: 76% of £82.

1% of £82 is 82p.

76% of £82 is 82p x 76 = 6232p = £62.32

Fractions and percentages 2 ~ Questions

1. Find:

a) $\frac{1}{3}$ of £450   b) $\frac{1}{8}$ of 96

c) $\frac{1}{6}$ of 72   d) $\frac{1}{5}$ of 105

2. Find:

a) $\frac{2}{3}$ of £450   b) $\frac{3}{5}$ of 20

c) $\frac{2}{7}$ of 35   d) $\frac{4}{9}$ of 117

3. A shop stocks 540 items.

$\frac{2}{3}$ of these were made in Britain. How many items were made in Britain?

4. There were 1000 cars in a car park.

$\frac{5}{8}$ of the cars were silver. How many silver cars were there in the car park?

5. Find:

a) 10% of 450   b) 15% of 500

c) 12% of 72   d) 70% of 105

6. Find:

a) 10% of £45   b) 15% of £35

c) 35% of £92   d) 20% of £40.50

7. In Sportsmart, Tom is given a 5% discount on a pair of trainers costing £45.
How much is the discount worth?

8. Abi earns £380 per week.
She gets a 7% pay rise.
By how much does her pay increase?

Fractions, decimals & percentages

You should know these:

$50\% = \frac{1}{2} = 0.5$ $25\% = \frac{1}{4} = 0.25$ $75\% = \frac{3}{4} = 0.75$

$33\frac{1}{3}\% = \frac{1}{3} = 0.3\dot{3}$ $66\frac{2}{3}\% = \frac{2}{3} = 0.6\dot{6}$

A percentage can be written as a fraction with a denominator (bottom number) equal to 100.

$7\% = \frac{7}{100}$ $70\% = \frac{70}{100}$

To convert a percentage into a decimal ~ divide by 100.

E.g. $70\% = \frac{70}{100} = 70 \div 100 = 0.7$

To convert a decimal into a percentage ~ multiply by 100.

$0.6 = 0.6 \times 100\% = 60\%$
$0.03 = 0.03 \times 100\% = 3\%$

To change a fraction into a percentage ~ multiply by 100.

$\frac{5}{8} = \frac{5}{8} \times 100\% = \frac{500}{8}\% = 62.5\%$

Example:

Place in order of size starting with the smallest: 43% 0.45 $\frac{2}{5}$

Using percentages we have 43% $0.45 \times 100 = 45\%$ $\frac{2}{5} \times 100 = 40\%$

So the order is $\frac{2}{5}$, 43%, 0.45.

To write a quantity as a fraction of another

Jo had £120 in her savings. At the end of the year she received £8 interest. Calculate the interest as a fraction of the money she had saved.

As a fraction $\frac{8}{120} = \frac{\not{4} \times 2}{\not{4} \times 30} = \frac{2}{30}$.

Calculate the interest as a percentage of the money she had saved. Change the fraction into a percentage by multiplying by 100.

$\frac{8}{120} \times 100\% = \frac{80}{12} = \frac{20}{3} = 6\frac{2}{3}\%$

Fractions, decimals & percentages ~ Questions

1. Change the following percentages into fractions.

a) 40% b) 25% c) $33\frac{1}{3}\%$ d) 15%

e) 50% f) 72% g) 35% h) 48%

2. Change the following percentages into decimals.

a) 60% b) 50% c) 67% d) 15%

e) 40% f) 36% g) 5% h) 1%

3. Change the following decimals into percentages.

a) 0.4 b) 0.5 c) 0.35 d) 0.16

e) 0.01 f) $0.\dot{3}$ g) $0.\dot{6}$ h) 0.005

4. Change the following fractions into percentages.

a) $\frac{1}{2}$ b) $\frac{3}{4}$ c) $\frac{1}{3}$ d) $\frac{7}{10}$

e) $\frac{4}{5}$ f) $\frac{17}{20}$ g) $\frac{3}{8}$ h) $\frac{2}{3}$

5. Write the following numbers in order of size, smallest first.

$\frac{1}{2}$ $\frac{2}{5}$ 0.6 35% 0.4 23% 70% $\frac{5}{8}$

6. Ali wants to buy a car.

The price of the car is £5000.
The dealer wants a deposit of £400.
Calculate the deposit as a percentage of the cost of the car.

7. Alan bought a computer for £800.

He sold it to a friend for £320.
Work out his loss as a percentage of the cost of the computer.

8. Mona is recording the amount of rain that falls on her school.

She records rain on 18 days in November.
On what percentage of the days did rain fall?

Addition & subtraction of fractions

Fractions are like any other two numbers, but they seem to cause a lot of concern to many people.

Here is how you add two fractions:

$\frac{3}{5} + \frac{2}{7}$

We must make the **denominators** (bottom numbers) equal, then it is easy.

$\frac{3}{5} = \frac{6}{10} = \frac{9}{15} = \frac{12}{20} = \frac{15}{25} = \frac{18}{30} = \mathbf{\frac{21}{35}} = \frac{24}{40}$

These are all equivalent fractions equal to $\frac{3}{5}$.

$\frac{2}{7} = \frac{4}{14} = \frac{6}{21} = \frac{8}{28} = \mathbf{\frac{10}{35}} = \frac{12}{40}$ These are all equivalent fractions equal to $\frac{2}{7}$.

We can see that $\frac{3}{5}$ is equivalent to $\mathbf{\frac{21}{35}}$ and $\frac{2}{7}$ is equivalent to $\mathbf{\frac{10}{35}}$.

So $\frac{3}{5} + \frac{2}{7}$ is equal to $\mathbf{\frac{21}{35}} + \mathbf{\frac{10}{35}}$.

The bottom numbers are now equal.

So the answer to $\frac{3}{5} + \frac{2}{7}$ is $\mathbf{\frac{31}{35}}$.

When we do a **subtraction**, we use a very similar technique.

$\frac{3}{5} - \frac{2}{7}$

Again this only becomes easy if we make the denominators the same.

becomes

$\mathbf{\frac{21}{35}} - \mathbf{\frac{10}{35}}$

These have the same number as denominator.

so

$\frac{3}{5} - \frac{2}{7} = \mathbf{\frac{21}{35}} - \mathbf{\frac{10}{35}}$

$= \mathbf{\frac{11}{35}}$

Addition & subtraction of fractions ~ Questions

1. Write down three fractions each one of which is equivalent to:

a) $\frac{2}{5}$ b) $\frac{3}{4}$ c) $\frac{3}{10}$ d) $\frac{1}{7}$ e) $\frac{6}{11}$

2. Write down the lowest form of each of these five fractions:

a) $\frac{10}{30}$ b) $\frac{12}{24}$ c) $\frac{25}{30}$ d) $\frac{240}{360}$ e) $\frac{49}{70}$

3. Work out:

a) $\frac{1}{2} + \frac{1}{4}$ b) $\frac{1}{4} + \frac{1}{8}$ c) $\frac{1}{2} + \frac{2}{5}$ d) $\frac{2}{3} + \frac{1}{3}$

e) $\frac{2}{3} + \frac{1}{4}$ f) $\frac{3}{4} + \frac{2}{5}$ g) $\frac{5}{6} + \frac{1}{4}$ h) $\frac{2}{5} + \frac{4}{10}$

i) $\frac{3}{8} + \frac{1}{7}$ j) $\frac{7}{9} + \frac{2}{10}$ k) $\frac{3}{7} + \frac{2}{5}$ l) $\frac{3}{20} + \frac{2}{10}$

m) $\frac{4}{9} + \frac{3}{10}$ n) $\frac{5}{12} + \frac{17}{30}$ o) $\frac{8}{9} + \frac{1}{11}$ p) $\frac{7}{12} + \frac{15}{20}$

4. Work out:

a) $\frac{1}{2} - \frac{1}{4}$ b) $\frac{1}{4} - \frac{1}{8}$ c) $\frac{1}{2} - \frac{2}{5}$ d) $\frac{2}{3} - \frac{1}{3}$

e) $\frac{2}{3} - \frac{1}{4}$ f) $\frac{3}{4} - \frac{2}{5}$ g) $\frac{5}{6} - \frac{1}{4}$ h) $\frac{4}{9} - \frac{2}{5}$

i) $\frac{3}{8} - \frac{1}{7}$ j) $\frac{7}{9} - \frac{2}{10}$ k) $\frac{3}{7} - \frac{2}{5}$ l) $\frac{3}{20} - \frac{2}{10}$

m) $\frac{4}{9} - \frac{3}{10}$ n) $\frac{17}{30} - \frac{5}{12}$ o) $\frac{8}{9} - \frac{1}{11}$ p) $\frac{15}{20} - \frac{7}{12}$

5. Work out:

a) $\frac{1}{2} + \frac{1}{4} - \frac{1}{8}$ b) $\frac{2}{3} - \frac{1}{4} + \frac{1}{5}$ c) $\frac{2}{5} + \frac{1}{2} - \frac{1}{3}$ d) $\frac{3}{7} - \frac{1}{4} + \frac{2}{3}$

Multiplication & division of fractions

There cannot be anything much easier than multiplying two fractions together.

$$\frac{1}{2} \times \frac{3}{5} = \frac{3}{10}$$

The word **multiply** is very similar to the word **of**.

Sometimes it is possible to cancel out some of the numbers:

$$\frac{2}{3} \times \frac{9}{10} = \frac{\overset{1}{\cancel{2}}}{\underset{1}{\cancel{3}}} \times \frac{\overset{3}{\cancel{9}}}{\underset{5}{\cancel{10}}} = \mathbf{\frac{3}{5}}$$

Dividing by a fraction is a little more complicated. Here is an example:

$3 \div \mathbf{\frac{1}{2}}$ means

How many halves in 3. We can see this by pictures:

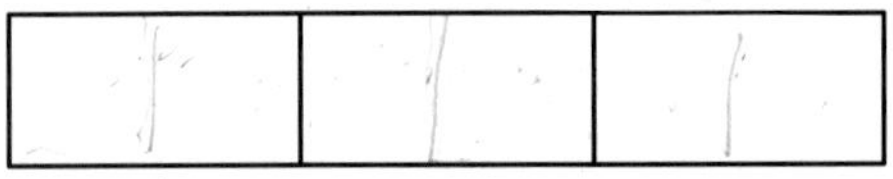

This is 3.

This is $\frac{1}{2}$.

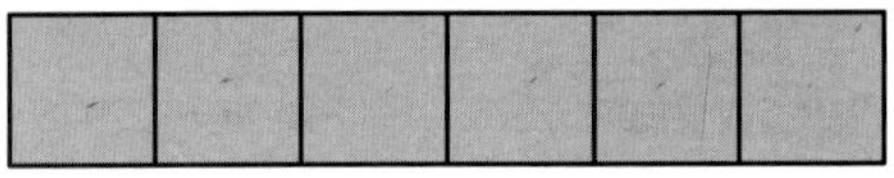

And there are **6** of  equal to 3.

So $\mathbf{3 \div \frac{1}{2} = 6}$

Which is precisely the same result as **3 x 2**

(**or** $\mathbf{3 \times \frac{2}{1}}$) (we just tip over $\frac{1}{2}$ and multiply)

Also $\mathbf{\frac{3}{5}} \div \mathbf{\frac{1}{2}}$ is $\frac{3}{5} \times \frac{2}{1} = \frac{3 \times 2}{5 \times 1} = \mathbf{\frac{6}{5}}$

Turn over $\frac{1}{2}$ and multiply.

Whilst $\mathbf{\frac{3}{4}} \div \mathbf{\frac{1}{2}}$ is $\frac{3}{4} \times \frac{2}{1} = \mathbf{\frac{3}{2}}$

This had some cancelling in it.

Multiplication & division of fractions ~ Questions

1. Work out:

a) $\frac{1}{3} \times 6$ b) $\frac{1}{3} \times 3$ c) $\frac{1}{4} \times 8$ d) $\frac{1}{7} \times 14$ e) $\frac{1}{10} \times 30$

f) $\frac{2}{5} \times 5$ g) $\frac{3}{7} \times 14$ h) $\frac{2}{5} \times 10$ i) $\frac{5}{6} \times 12$ j) $\frac{4}{10} \times 30$

2. Work out:

a) $\frac{2}{5} \times \frac{3}{4}$ b) $\frac{1}{5} \times \frac{5}{7}$ c) $\frac{3}{10} \times \frac{5}{12}$ d) $\frac{4}{7} \times \frac{3}{14}$ e) $\frac{3}{7} \times \frac{7}{12}$

f) $\frac{3}{5} \times \frac{3}{5}$ g) $\frac{4}{5} \times \frac{5}{8}$ h) $\frac{2}{9} \times \frac{3}{4}$ i) $\frac{5}{12} \times \frac{6}{11}$ j) $\frac{12}{15} \times \frac{10}{15}$

k) $\frac{3}{5} \times \frac{5}{6}$ l) $\frac{5}{8} \times \frac{7}{10}$ m) $\frac{3}{4} \times \frac{8}{9}$ n) $\frac{2}{7} \times \frac{7}{10}$ o) $\frac{14}{15} \times \frac{15}{16}$

p) $\frac{6}{34} \times \frac{17}{18}$ q) $\frac{1}{4} \times \frac{10}{19}$ r) $\frac{12}{15} \times \frac{17}{18}$ s) $\frac{15}{16} \times \frac{1}{3}$ t) $\frac{3}{5} \times \frac{2}{3}$

3. Work out:

a) $4 \div \frac{1}{2}$ b) $5 \div \frac{1}{3}$ c) $2 \div \frac{1}{3}$ d) $3 \div \frac{1}{5}$ e) $2 \div \frac{1}{6}$

f) $6 \div \frac{2}{3}$ g) $1 \div \frac{1}{4}$ h) $3 \div \frac{2}{3}$ i) $5 \div \frac{5}{6}$ j) $4 \div \frac{2}{3}$

4. Work out:

a) $\frac{4}{5} \div \frac{1}{2}$ b) $\frac{5}{6} \div \frac{1}{3}$ c) $\frac{2}{3} \div \frac{1}{3}$ d) $\frac{3}{5} \div \frac{1}{5}$ e) $\frac{2}{9} \div \frac{1}{6}$

f) $\frac{6}{5} \div \frac{2}{3}$ g) $\frac{1}{8} \div \frac{1}{4}$ h) $\frac{3}{5} \div \frac{2}{3}$ i) $\frac{5}{6} \div \frac{5}{6}$ j) $\frac{4}{7} \div \frac{2}{3}$

k) $\frac{2}{3} \div \frac{3}{7}$ l) $\frac{5}{8} \div \frac{7}{6}$ m) $\frac{13}{4} \div \frac{8}{3}$ n) $\frac{3}{5} \div \frac{4}{7}$ o) $\frac{5}{8} \div \frac{8}{12}$

p) $\frac{3}{8} \div \frac{9}{7}$ q) $\frac{4}{5} \div \frac{2}{7}$ r) $\frac{8}{1} \div \frac{5}{2}$ s) $\frac{13}{15} \div \frac{7}{10}$ t) $\frac{15}{21} \div \frac{14}{3}$

Ratio and proportion

Here is a rectangle. It is made from 18 squares.
Six of the squares are **shaded** and twelve of the squares are unshaded.

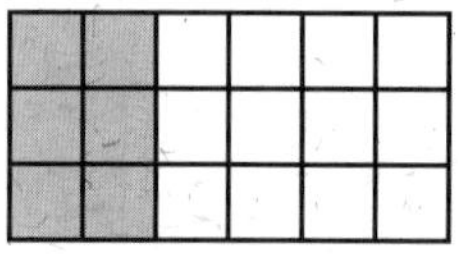

The **ratio** of the **shaded squares** to the **unshaded squares** is:

6 : 12

The ratio can be **simplified**:

$$\begin{aligned} & 6 : 12 \\ = {} & 3 \times 2 : 3 \times 4 = 3 \times 2 : 3 \times 4 \\ = {} & 2 : 4 \end{aligned}$$

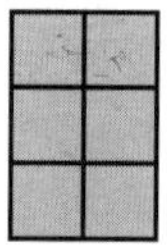

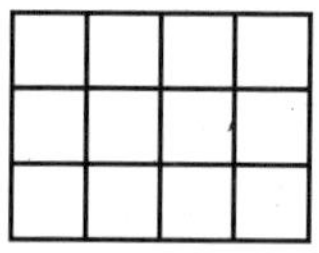

This can be further **simplified**:

$$\begin{aligned} & 2 : 4 \\ = {} & 2 \times 1 : 2 \times 2 = 2 \times 1 : 2 \times 2 \\ = {} & 1 : 2 \end{aligned}$$

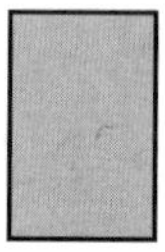

This cannot be simplified any more. It is in its **lowest terms**.

The ratios 6 : 12 and 2 : 4 and 1 : 2 are all equal but

1 : 2

is the ratio in its lowest terms.

Two **numbers** are **in proportion** if their ratio stays the same as each number gets either bigger or smaller.

Imagine that Shadwell School has **40** teachers and **1000** students. The ratio of students to teachers is 1000 : 40 or 25 : 1. This means that for every **25** students there is **1** teacher.

Suppose that Shadwell School doubled in size, so its new population is **2000** students. To keep the **ratio** of students to teachers the same as before there would need to be 2 x 40 = **80 teachers**.

Ratio and proportion ~ Questions

1. **Write down the ratio of the shaded parts to the unshaded parts in each of these cases.**
Write each ratio in its lowest terms.

a) 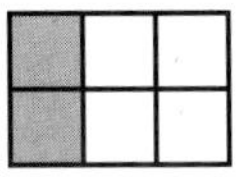

b) 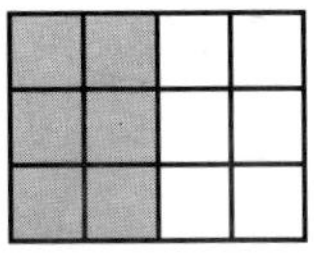

c) 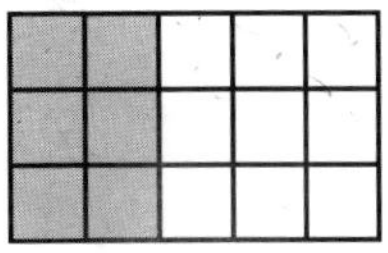

d) 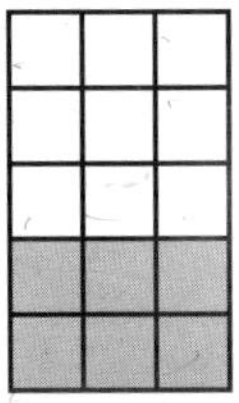

e) 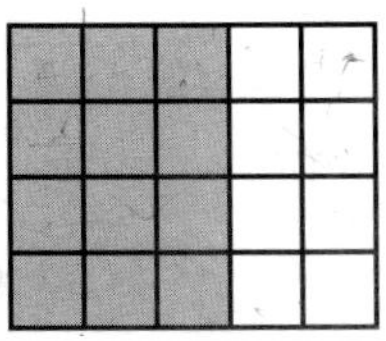

f) 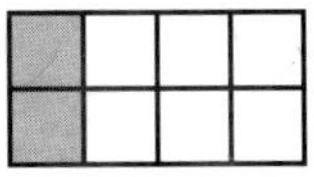

g) 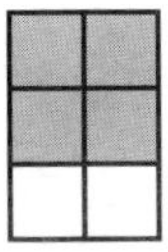

h) 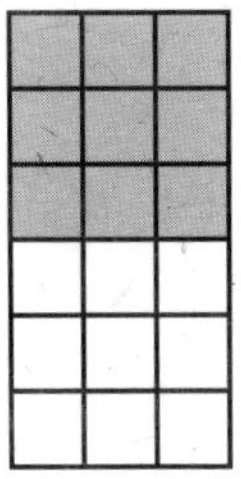

2. **Write each of these ratios in its lowest terms.**

a) 4 : 12 b) 5 : 10 c) 3 : 15 d) 8 : 20

e) 9 : 36 f) 15 : 20 g) 24 : 12 h) 30 : 5

i) 42 : 14 j) 12 : 100 k) 18 : 45 l) 60 : 100

3. **Peter is exactly 7 years older than his sister.**

Write down, in its lowest terms, the ratio of Peter's age to his sister's age when Peter is aged:

a) 14 years b) 21 years c) 42 years d) 70 years

4. **Mrs Kayten won £360 in a raffle.**

She shared the money between herself and her daughter in the ratio
Mrs Katen's share : Her daughter's share = 5 : 1

How much was: a) Mrs Kayten's share?

b) Her daughter's share?

5. **A builder has two piles of bricks.**

The numbers of bricks in each pile are in the ratio 6 : 1.
There are 300 bricks in the larger pile.
How many bricks are there in the smaller pile.

Number patterns

Here is a pattern of shapes made out of matchsticks:

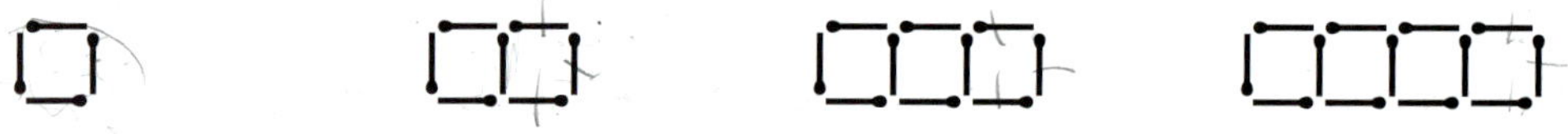

Pattern 1	Pattern 2	Pattern 3	Pattern 4
4 matchsticks	7 matchsticks	10 matchsticks	13 matchsticks

This gives us a number pattern of **4 7 10 13** (+3, +3, +3)

The rule to move from one shape to the next is '**add three**'.

Odd numbers

These are the numbers 1, 3, 5, 7, 8, 9, 11...

They go up by two each time but they are not divisible by 2.

Even numbers

These are the numbers 2, 4, 6, 8, 10, 12...

These also go up by two a time and they are all divisible by 2.

Multiples

15 = 5 x 3

15 is the fifth multiple of 3.

Here is the start of the multiples of 3:

> 15 = 3 x 5
> So 15 is also the third multiple of 5.

3	6	9	12	15	18
1 x 3	2 x 3	3 x 3	4 x 3	5 x 3	6 x 3

Factors

The number 28 has factors of: 1, 2, 4, 7, 14, 28.

These are called factors because:

28 = 1 x 28   28 = 2 x 14   28 = 4 x 7

A number which divides into a second number an exact number of times is called a factor of the second number.

The square numbers

These are the first five square numbers:

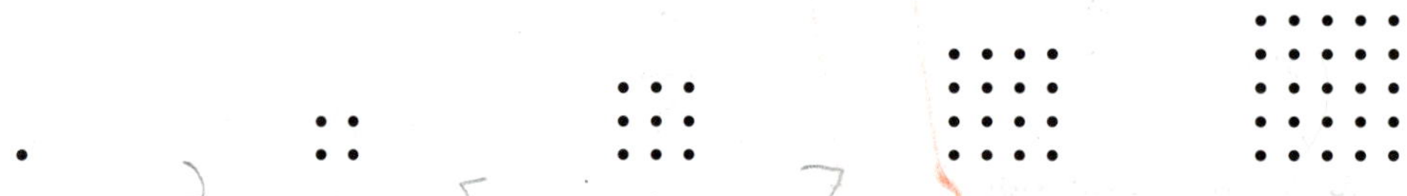

1	4	9	16	25
1 = 1 x 1	4 = 2 x 2	9 = 3 x 3	16 = 4 x 4	25 = 5 x 5
$1 = 1^2$	$4 = 2^2$	$9 = 3^2$	$16 = 4^2$	$25 = 5^2$

Number patterns ~ Questions

1. Write down:

a) The last **odd** number before 20

b) The first **even** number after 40

c) A **square** number which is **even**

d) **A factor** of 12 which is **odd**

2. Which of these numbers are:

a) multiples of 3: 18, 9, 3, 14, 15

b) multiples of 7: 15, 8, 14, 21, 23

c) multiples of both 4 and 6: 8, 15, 12, 18, 24

3. Write down the next two numbers in each pattern:

a) 5, 8, 11, 14, 17

b) 9, 13, 17, 21, 25

c) 100, 97, 94, 91, 88

d) 1, 7, 13, 19, 25

e) 3, 6, 10, 15, 21

f) 1, 2, 4, 8, 16

4. Copy and complete this table of numbers:

Number	1	2	3	4	5		7	8	
Number square	1	4		16		36			

5. Write down the factors of:

a) 14

b) 56

c) 72

d) 100

e) 360

6. Work out:

a) $6^2 + 8^2$

b) $5^2 + 12^2$

c) $17^2 - 8^2$

7. a) i) Work out the value of $3^2 + 4^2$.

ii) Find the value of x so that $3^2 + 4^2 = x^2$.

b) i) Work out the value of $10^2 + 24^2$.

ii) Find the value of $26^2 - 24^2$.

Sequences

Number patterns written in order are called sequences.

Common sequences you should recognise:

whole numbers	1, 2, 3, 4, ...
even numbers	2, 4, 6, 8, 10, ...
odd numbers	1, 3, 5, 7, 9, ...
multiples of 3	1, 3, 6, 9, 12, ...
multiples of 7	1, 7, 14, 21, 28, ...
prime numbers	2, 3, 5, 7, 11, ...
square numbers	1, 4, 9, 16, 25, ...

Each number in the sequence is called a term.
The terms are numbered.

To find the 5th term in the sequence: 9, 18, 27, 36, 45, 54, 63, ...

Term number	*1st, 2nd, 3rd, 4th, 5th, 6th, 7th, ...*
Term	9, 18, 27, 36, 45, 54, 63, ...

So the 5th term is 45.

To find the nth term in the sequence: 9, 18, 27, 36, 45, 54, 63, ...
We need to identify the pattern. Notice the terms seem to look like the 9 times table!

Term number (n)	*1st, 2nd, 3rd, 4th, 5th, 6th, 7th,*
Term	9, 18, 27, 36, 45, 54, 63, ...

The sequence with nth term $9n$ would give us:

Term number (n)	*1st, 2nd, 3rd, 4th, 5th, 6th, 7th,*
Term	9, 18, 27, 36, 45, 54, 63, ...

The sequence is $9n$.

To find the nth term in the sequence: 7, 16, 25, 34, ...

Term number (n)	*1st, 2nd, 3rd, 4th, 5th, 6th, 7th,*
Term	7, 16, 25, 34, ...

The terms go up in 9s, so consider the 9 times table:

Term number (n)	*1st, 2nd, 3rd, 4th, 5th, 6th, 7th,*
Term	7, 16, 25, 34, 43, 52, ...
$9n$	9, 18, 27, 36, 45, 54, ...

The nth term will be $9n - 2$.

You may be given diagrams.

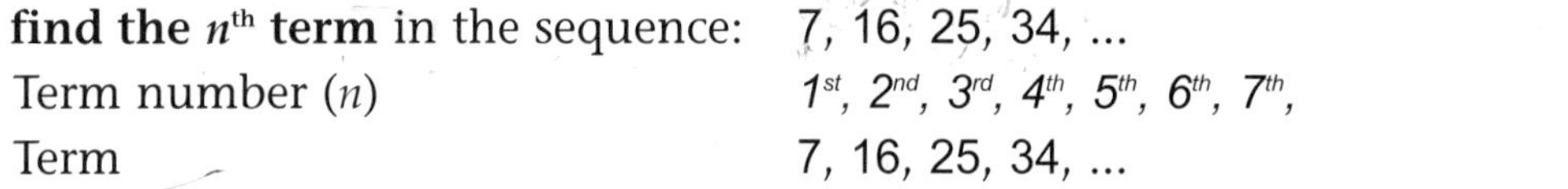

Alan has made a pattern from some octagons.
The number of outside edges form a number pattern: 8, 14, 20, 26, ...
The numbers go up in 6s. The next term will be 32.
The nth term will be $6n + 2$.

Sequences ~ Questions

1. Here are the first 5 numbers in some simple sequences:

a) 5 9 13 17 21 b) 7 12 17 22 27

c) 1 2 4 7 11 d) 22 20 18 16 14

Write down the next term in each of the sequences.

2. The following sequence has some numbers missing from the pattern.

2 6 .... 18 22 26

a) Fill in the missing numbers.
b) Write down the rule you used to find the missing numbers.

3. Here is a sequence of numbers:

7 10 13 16 19

a) Find the next term in the sequence.
b) Find the 10th term of the sequence.
c) Explain the rule you used to find the nth term.
d) Find the nth term of the sequence.

4. Here are the first 5 terms of a number sequence:

20 17 14 11 8

a) Find the next term in the sequence.
b) Explain the rule you used to find the next term.
c) Find the nth term of the sequence.

5. David is making a chain.

He uses silver rods to make a sequence of hexagons as shown in the diagram below.

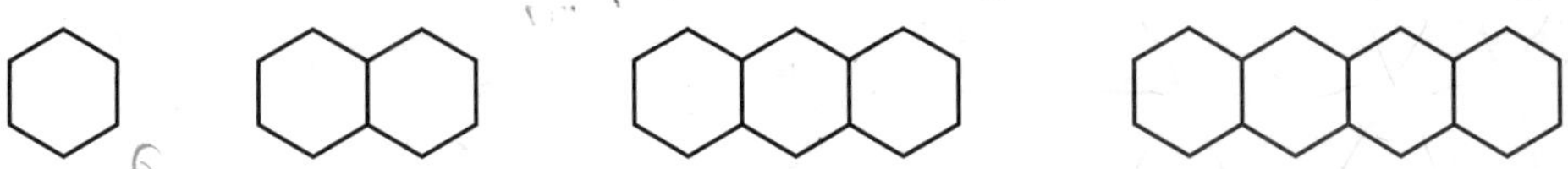

a) Draw a diagram to show the number of rods needed for 5 hexagons.
b) Explain how you would work out the number for 10 hexagons without drawing a diagram.
c) Copy and complete the table below showing the number of rods needed for different numbers of hexagons.

Number of Hexagons	1	2	3	4	5	6	7	8
Number of rods	6	11	16	21				

d) The number of rods needed forms a number sequence.
Write down an expression for the nth term in the sequence.

Negative numbers

Numbers greater than (>) 0 are positive numbers.

Numbers less than (<) 0 are negative numbers.

These are **directed** numbers.

–4 –3 –2 –1 0 1 2 3 4

Negative numbers are smaller than positive numbers!

$-4 < 0 \qquad 4 > -1$

Numbers without a sign are assumed to be positive: 7 means +7
Think of cheques and bills going into a bank account.
Cheques are positive, bills are negative!

2 cheques paid in:
one for +7 and one for +3 means you have +10.

$+7 + (+3) = 10$

If you had +7 before you were given
a bill for 3. You have +4

$+7+(-3) = 4$

If you owed 6 and then are given a cheque for 2, you still owe 4.

$-6 + (+2) = -4$

If you owe 9 and now another bill for 4 arrives, you owe 13.

$-9 + (-4) = -13$

If you have 7 and then take away a cheque for 9:
this is more than you have, so you end up owing 2.

$+7 - (+9) = -2$

If you have 7 and then take away a bill for 9:
this is more than you have so you end up owing 2.

$+7 - (-9) = 16$

If you have a bill for 7 and then take away a bill for 9:
this leaves you better off by 2.

$-7 - (-9) = 2$

Negative numbers ~ Questions

1. Copy the number line and fill in the missing numbers.

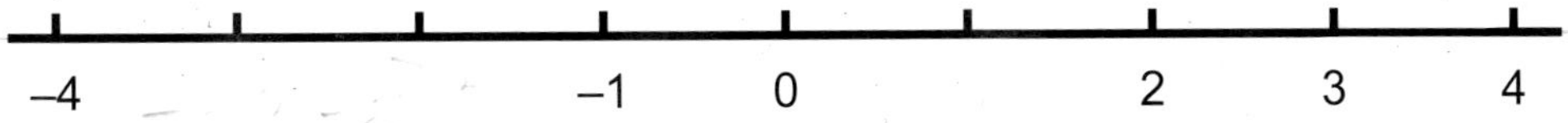

2. Arrange these temperatures in order of size, smallest first.

–1°C –10°C 3°C –4°C 2°C –6°C

3. The temperature in Moscow was –10°C.

If it rose to 5°C, by how many degrees would the temperature have risen?

4. a) +5 + (+4) = b) +7 + (–6) = c) –9 + (+6) =

d) –8 + (–4) = e) –4 + (–3) = f) 6 + (– 9) =

g) 8 + (–3) = h) –6 + 3 = i) –3 + 7 =

j) +5 – (+6) = k) +6 – (–3) = l) –5 – (+4) =

m) –9 – (–3) = n) 8 – (–6) = o) 3 – (–5) =

p) –3 – 5 = q) 4 – (+3) = r) –2 – (+3) =

5. Two counters are dropped onto this board.

The player scores by adding together the numbers of the squares in which the counter lands.

Write down all of the possible scores.

–2	4
3	–5

6. Arrange these temperatures in order of size.

Start with the smallest.

–6°C 5°C 0°C –8°C 4°C

Expressions and formulae

In **algebra** we often use **letters** to stand for numbers.

$x + 3$ means 3 more than x.

$5 \times y$ becomes $5y$.

Usually we do not write a x sign.

This is how we write a number take away 2: $n - 2$

This is how we write a number divided by 2. $\frac{p}{2}$

These four pieces of algebra:

$x + 3$

$5y$

$n - 2$

$\frac{p}{2}$

are all called **expressions**.

Sometimes we can simplify an expression.

$n + n + n + n$ This is 4 times n, which is = $4n$.

Whilst $8m - 2m = 6m$.

A **formula** connects two letters:

$y = x + 3$ is a formula.

You can work out the value of y when you are told the value of x:

	$y = x + 3$
When	$x = 5$
	$y = 5 + 3$
So	$y = 8$

This is one of the most common uses of a formula.

Algebra 1

Expressions and formulae ~ Questions

1. Write down an expression for each of these numbers.

a) 4 more than x
b) y take away 5
c) z minus 1
d) t divided by 4
e) one divided by w
f) twice x
g) three times p
h) 5 multiplied by s
i) four times y
j) seven less than q
k) x divided by y
l) three times p then add 2

2. The sum of two numbers is 10. One of the numbers is n.

Write down an expression for the other number.

3. There are b boys and 8 girls in a youth club.

Write down an expression for the total number of members at the youth club.

4. City scored seven goals more than United. City scored x goals.

Write down an expression for the number of goals scored by United.

5. Jackie is aged y years. Her mother is three times Jackie's age.

Write down an expression for her mother's age.

6. Terry has n pounds. He spends one third of it.

Write down an expression for the amount he has left.

7. Simplify each expression.

a) $x + x + x$
b) $y + y + y + y + y$
c) $p + p$
d) $r + r + r - r$
e) $t + t - t + t + t$
f) $4x + 3x$
g) $8m - m$
h) $14q - 5q$
i) $11t + 2t$
j) $3r + r - r$
k) $2t - t$
l) $s + 3s + 2s$

8. There are n cars parked in a car park. Each car has 4 wheels.

Write down a formula for w, the total number of wheels in the car park.

9. Here are some patterns made from matchsticks.

Pattern 1 Pattern 2 Pattern 3

a) How many matchsticks will there be in:

i) Pattern 4
ii) Pattern 10

b) Write down a formula for m, the number of matchsticks used in Pattern n.

Constructing algebraic expressions & formulae

A piece of ribbon is $x$cm long.
10cm is cut from the end of the ribbon.
Write an expression for the length of ribbon left.

An expression for the length is $x - 10$.

$h$cm

Write an expression for a trophy twice as high as this.

An expression for the height of the larger trophy is $2h$.

A telephone company makes a 25p connection charge plus 5p for every minute (m) Tom spends on the phone.
Write down an expression for the cost of a call.

An expression for the cost of a call (in pence) is $25 + 5m$.

Bill is $t$cm tall. Sue's height is $t - 3$, which means Sue is 3cm shorter than Bill.

Joe's height is $t + 4$, which means Joe is 4cm taller than Bill.

Ann's height is $\frac{1}{2}h$, which means Ann is half as tall as Bill.

A **formula** has an equals sign.

A telephone company makes a 25p connection charge plus 5p for every minute (m) spent making the call.

Write down an expression for the cost of a call:

an expression for the cost of a call is $25 + 5m$.

Write down a formula for the cost C of a call:

a formula for the cost of a call is $C = 25 + 5m$.

Constructing algebraic expressions & formulae ~ Questions

1. There are 25 seats in a row at the cinema.

a) How many seats are there in 10 rows?

b) How many seats in n rows?

2. Jane is 14 years old.

a) How old will she be in 3 years?

b) How old will she be in x years?

3. The diagram shows a regular hexagon of side s cm.

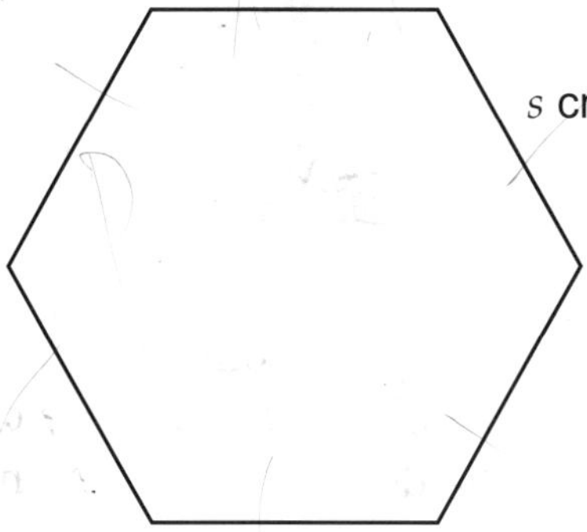

a) Write down an expression for the perimeter of the hexagon.

b) Write down a formula for P the perimeter of the hexagon.

4. n is a number.

Use n to write down expressions for the following:

a) the sum of the number and 1

b) five times the number

c) 4 less than the number

d) half of the number

5. Amy is x years old.

a) Write down a formula for T ~ the age of Tom ~ who is twice as old as Amy.

b) Write down a formula for M ~ the age of Mark ~ who is 4 years older than Amy.

c) Write down a formula for A ~ the age of Amy ~ in 3 years time.

Jim is 3 times as old as Amy today.

d) Write down a formula for J ~ Jims's age ~ in 3 years time.

Using formulae

Here is a formula:

$A = B + 6$

Find the value of A when $B = 2$.

Replace the letter with the number it represents.

$A = B + 6$ If $B = 2$ then $A = 2 + 6$
so $A = 8$

This formula gives the height H, in cm, of a bookcase made up of a frame of height 30cm and then 45cm for each shelf s in the bookcase.

$H = 30 + 45s$

Find the height of a bookcase with 4 shelves.

$H = 30 + 45s$ – when $s = 4$

$H = 30 + 45 \times 4$
$H = 30 + 180$
$H = 210\text{cm}$

The cost £C of a take away meal of fish and chips is given by the formula

£$C = 3.5f + 1.5c$

Where f is the number of pieces of fish and c is the number of scoops of chips.
Use this formula to find the cost of 5 pieces of fish and 10 scoops of chips: £$C = 3.5 \times 5 + 1.5 \times 10 =$ £32.50

The formula for the perimeter P of a rectangle is given by

$P = 2(w + h)$

where w is the width and h is the height of the rectangle.
Use this formula to work out the perimeter of a rectangle with width 3 and height 4cm.

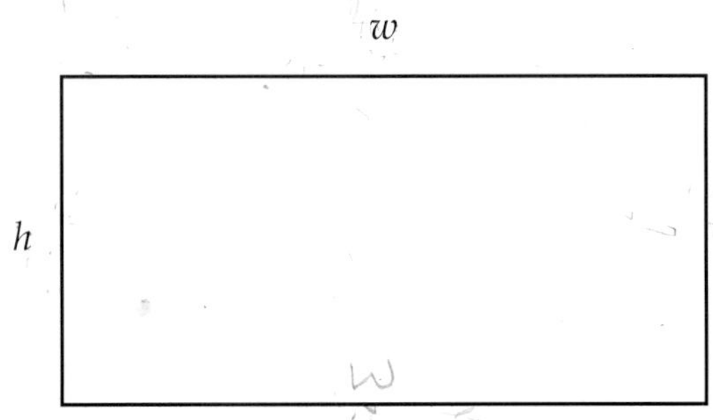

$P = 2(3 + 4)$

$= 14\text{cm}$

Using formulae ~ Questions

1. A salesman earns a basic wage of £200 per week, plus an extra £20 for each computer he sells.

His weekly salary (£S) is given by the formula

£$S = 200 + 20c$

Where c is the number of computers sold.

How much is his weekly salary (£S) if he sells:

a) 5 computers b) no computers

c) 12 computers d) 9 computers

2. The growth of a plant is dependent on temperature.

The warmer it is, the faster the plant grows.

Jane worked out the formula for the height H (in cm) of a plant kept at a constant temperature $t°$ for 2 weeks.

$H = 10 + 0.6t$

Find the height of the plant (in cm) if the temperature was:

a) 10° b) 0° c) 15° d) 20°

3. The perimeter P of a regular polygon of side 5cm is given by $P = 5s$ where s is the number of sides.

Copy and complete the table for regular polygons of side 5cm.

Sides (s)	3	4	5	6	8
Perimeter (P)					

4. Given that $v = u + ft$:

Work out the value of v when:

a) $u = 30$, $f = 2$, $t = 25$

b) $u = 40$, $f = -6$, $t = 10$

c) $u = -10$, $f = 4$, $t = 20$

Simplifying expressions

$3ab$ means $3 \times a \times b$ which is exactly the same as $a \times 3 \times b$ or $b \times a \times 3$.

We write algebraic expressions:

- without the x sign;
- numbers at the front;
- in alphabetical order.

$a \times a$ is written a^2.

Simplify the expression means to write it in a neater form.

Simplify: $6 \times a$ The answer is $6a$.

$7a \times a$ The answer is $7a^2$.

$2a \times 5b$ The answer is $10ab$.

Expressions may be added or subtracted.

Simplify: $5n + 4n$ The answer is $9n$.

$5n - n$ The answer is $4n$.

A letter n without a number means $1n$. More shorthand!

To remove brackets, multiply everything inside the bracket by the number or letters outside.

$$3(a + 4) = 3 \times a + 3 \times 4$$
$$= 3a + 12$$

$$4(a - 2) = 4 \times a - 4 \times 2$$
$$= 4a - 8$$

$$5(2a - 3) = 5 \times 2a - 5 \times 3$$
$$= 10a - 15$$

$$-2(3a + 4) = -2 \times 3a + -2 \times 4$$
$$= -6a + -8$$
$$= -6a - 8$$

$$-3(4a - 2) = -3 \times 4a - -3 \times 2$$
$$= -12a + 6$$

Remove the brackets and simplify:

$$3(x + 2) + 2(x + 1) = 3x + 6 + 2x + 2$$
$$= 3x + 2x + 6 + 2$$
$$= 5x + 8$$

$$2(3 - 2a) + 4(5 + a) = 6 - 4a + 20 + 4a$$
$$= 6 + 20 - 4a + 4a$$
$$= 26$$

Simplifying expressions ~ Questions

1. Simplify these expressions:

a) $2 \times p \times q$ b) $3 \times a \times a$ c) $2 \times a \times b$

d) $2 \times q + 3 \times r$ e) $5n + 3n$ f) $7y - y$

2. Simplify these expressions:

a) $5a - 2a + 3a$ b) $3a + 2a + m + 3m$

c) $5a + 2b + 3a + 4b$ d) $4a + 2b - 3a - b$

e) $3a + 2b - 4a + b$ f) $5a - 4m - a - 2m$

3. Write the following expressions without brackets:

a) $2(x + 4)$ b) $4(a - 5)$ c) $3(2p + q)$

d) $3(x - 3y)$ e) $-2(x + 3)$ f) $-3(x - 4)$

4. Remove the brackets and simplify:

a) $3(x + 2) + 2(x + 4)$ b) $4(y - 1) + 5$

c) $2(3p - 1) + 4(p + 2)$ d) $5(3a - 2) + 2(2a - 6)$

e) $3(2q + 4) - 2(q + 6)$ f) $4(2a - 3) - 3(3a + 4)$

g) $5(3q + 4) - 4(4q - 2)$ h) $3(g - 2) - 4(2g - 5)$

5. Copy this table to help you to decode the message:

9	7	1	5	10	6	9	11	3	12	11	4	2	8

The expressions in the first box can be simplified to give an answer from the second box. Use these answers to decode the message.

1	$2(3a + 1)$	**7**	$4 \times a - 2$
2	$4 \times s$	**8**	$5a + 3a$
3	$w + w$	**9**	$5a - 4a$
4	$4(a - 2)$	**10**	$2 \times y$
5	$y \times y$	**11**	$3(a - 2) - 7$
6	$3(2a - 4b)$	**12**	$3(a + 2) - 7$

a	a	**l**	$4a - 2$
b	$2y$	**n**	$8a$
e	y^2	**r**	$6a - 12b$
f	$4a - 8$	**s**	$3a - 1$
g	$6a + 2$	**u**	$4s$
i	$2w$	**t**	$3a - 13$

Solving linear equations 1

Alan thinks of a number.
He then adds on seven.
This gives him a result of ten.

?
? + 7 = 10
? = 3

What number did he think of?

The answer is 3.

Here is the way to do this question, using **Algebra**.

Let n be the number.

Alan thinks of a number.
He then adds on seven.

This gives him a result of ten.

So the number he was thinking of must have been 3 because 3 + 7 = 10.

Write the number as n.
So he has $n + 7$.

So $n + 7 = 10$

$n + 7 = 10$
$n = 10 - 7$
$n = 3$

Sarah thinks of a number.
She multiplies it by four.
This gives her a result of twenty-four.
What number did she originally think of?

?
4 x ?
4 x ? = 24
? = 6

Here is a way to do this problem, using **Algebra**.

Sarah thinks of a number.
She multiplies it by four.
Which is written as $4m$.
This gives her a result of 24.

The answer will be 6 because 24 ÷ 4 = 6.

Write the number as m.
So this is 4 x m.
So $4m = 24$.

So $4 \times m = 24$
$m = 24 \div 4$ so $m = 6$

Now here is a way to do one of these equations using **algebra**.

Solve:	$3p = 12$	Think of a number, multiply it by 3 to give us 12.
	$P = 12 \div 3$	The number is 12 ÷ 3 = 4.
	$p = 4$	The equation is solved.

Algebra 2

Solving linear equations 1 ~ Questions

1. Write each one of these as a mathematical equation:

Use any letter to stand for a number. Solve the equation you obtain.

a) Georgina thinks of a number.
She adds two.
The result is five.
What number did Georgina think of?

b) Tim thinks of a number.
He adds four.
The result is twelve.
What number did Tim think of.

c) James thinks of a number.
He divides it by three.
The result is two.
What number did James think of?

d) Ann thinks of a number.
She takes it away from ten.
The result is four.
What number did Ann think of?

e) Kerry thinks of a number.
She multiplies it by five.
The result is forty.
What number did Kerry think of?

f) Peter thinks of a number.
He takes away three.
The result is nine.
What number did Peter think of?

g) Eric is 3 years older than Jane.
Jane is aged 14.
How old is Eric?

h) The distance around a square is 12cm. Work out the length of a side of the square.

2. Solve each of these equations:

a) $y + 2 = 5$ b) $n + 3 = 7$ c) $x - 4 = 5$

d) $3 + p = 9$ e) $8 - m = 1$ f) $5 + t = 12$

g) $r - 2 = 6$ h) $z + 13 = 21$ i) $20 - q = 8$

j) $s + 16 = 27$ k) $w - 1 = 1$ l) $31 - u = 17$

3. Solve each of these equations:

a) $3x = 21$ b) $2p = 10$ c) $y \div 3 = 2$

d) $5n = 15$ e) $\frac{m}{2} = 3$ f) $\frac{q}{2} = 5$

g) $2r = 7$ h) $4s = -12$ i) $3t = -6$

j) $3z = 4\frac{1}{2}$ k) $\frac{5w}{2} = 10$ l) $\frac{2v}{3} = 8$

NB: $\frac{m}{2}$ means the same as $m \div 2$. $\frac{5w}{2}$ means the same as $(5 \times w) \div 2$.

Solving linear equations 2

Solve equations by breaking the work down into small steps.

$7x - 1 = 20$

$7x = 20 + 1$

> First find $7x$.
> Undo the -1 by adding 1 to both sides.

$7x = 21$

$x = 21 \div 7$

> Now we have $7x$ or 7 times x.
> Undo $7x$ by dividing by 7.

$x = 3$

The answers are not always whole numbers.

$3y + 2 = 4$

$3y = 4 - 2$

$3y = 2$

$y = \frac{2}{3}$

> **Leave your answer as a fraction.**

There may be letters on both sides of the equation.

$5x + 7 = 2x - 1$

> Rearrange the equation to place all of the x terms on the same side.

$5x - 2x + 7 = -1$

$3x + 7 = -1$

> Work out the x terms: $5x - 2x = 3x$.
> Rearrange the equation to place all of the numbers without a letter on the same side.

$3x = -1 - 7$

$3x = -8$

$x = -\frac{8}{3} = -2\frac{2}{3}$

> Work out the numbers $-1 - 7 = -8$.
> Undo times 3.
> **Leave your answer as a fraction.**

$3n + 4$

$n \times 3$ or $3n$

Jane has a secret number. She multiplies it by 3.
She then adds 4.
The answer is 31.
Can you find her secret number.

$3n + 4 = 31$

$3n + 4 = 31 \quad 3n = 31 - 4 \quad 3n = 27 \quad n = 9$

Solving linear equations 2 ~ Questions

1. a) $3x + 2 = 8$ b) $5x - 4 = 31$ c) $7x + 1 = 22$

d) $4y - 5 = 9$ e) $9c - 2 = 34$ f) $3c - 6 = 0$

g) $6y - 2 = 10$ h) $8 - x = 3$ i) $7 - 2x = 1$

2. a) $5x - 3 = 1$ b) $3x + 6 = 7$ c) $7y - 1 = 3$

d) $4t + 4 = 11$ e) $6y + 2 = 7$ f) $2z - 1 = 4$

g) $9x + 4 = 10$ h) $9 - 2x = 4$ i) $2 - 3x = 6$

3. a) $5x - 3 = 2x + 6$ b) $3x + 7 = x - 1$ c) $7y - 3 = y + 3$

d) $4b + 4 = b - 2$ e) $6y + 7 = 2y - 3$ f) $3z - 1 = z + 4$

g) $9x + 4 = 5x - 2$ h) $2x + 3 = 5x - 2$ i) $6x - 7 = 3x - 2$

4. Mike has a secret number.

He multiplies it by 6.
He then adds 5.
The answer is 29.
Find Mike's secret number.

5. The diagram shows a triangle with sides x, $x + 1$ and $x + 2$.

The perimeter of the triangle is 17cm.

a) Find the length of the shortest side.

b) Find the length of the longest side.
Give answers correct to 2dp.

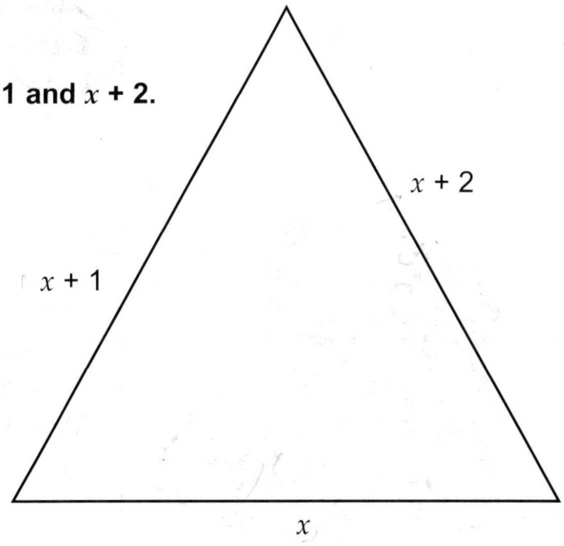

Solving linear equations 3

Some equations include brackets.

$3(4x + 2) = 10$

You will have to expand the brackets.

$12x + 6 = 10$

This is the same as the equations we can already do!!

$12x = 10 - 6$

$12x = 4$

$x = \frac{1}{3}$

Fractions are not difficult...

$\frac{2x}{3} + 6 = 2x$

If we multiply everything on both sides by 3 the expressions will still be equal but they will be easier to solve.

$2x + 18 = 6x$

$18 = 6x - 2x$

$18 = 4x$

These two are the same equation!!

$4x = 18$

$x = \frac{18}{4} = \frac{9}{2} = 4\frac{1}{2}$

An x on the bottom can be dealt with in the same way!

$\frac{x + 3}{2x} = 5$

If we multiply everything on both sides by $2x$ the expressions will still be equal but they will be easier to solve.

$x + 3 = 10x$

$3 = 9x$

$9x = 3$

$x = \frac{3}{9} = \frac{1}{3}$

Solving linear equations 3 ~ Questions

1. Solve the following equations:

a) $4(x + 2) = 20$ b) $3(x - 6) = 21$ c) $7(x + 1) = 28$

d) $3(2x + 1) = 15$ e) $9(3x - 1) = 45$ f) $8(4x - 2) = 80$

g) $4(x + 3) = 9$ h) $5(2x + 2) = 7$ i) $6(3x + 2) = 10$

2. The following equations involve fractions. Solve the equations.

a) $\frac{x + 2}{3} = 4$ b) $\frac{3x + 5}{4} = 5$ c) $\frac{3x - 2}{7} = 8$

d) $\frac{x}{3} + 4 = 5$ e) $\frac{3x}{4} + 5 = 7$ f) $\frac{8x}{7} - 2 = 3$

g) $\frac{4x}{5} - 3 = 13$ h) $\frac{6x}{9} + 4 = \frac{1}{3}$ i) $5 - \frac{3x}{8} = 2$

3. Show your working when you solve these equations:

a) $\frac{3}{x} = 2$ b) $\frac{8}{3x} = 2$ c) $\frac{9}{4x} = 12$

d) $\frac{4}{2x} + 1 = 6$ e) $\frac{7}{3x} - 4 = 7$ f) $\frac{8}{3x} - 4 = 9$

g) $\frac{3}{x - 1} = 2$ h) $\frac{4}{3x + 2} = 6$ i) $\frac{8}{2x - 3} = 4$

j) $\frac{x + 1}{x + 2} = 6$ k) $\frac{2x + 1}{3x + 2} = 4$ l) $\frac{2x - 1}{4x - 2} = 7$

m) $\frac{2x + 4}{x - 1} = \frac{1}{2}$ n) $\frac{5x - 2}{3x + 4} = \frac{1}{4}$ o) $\frac{6x - 3}{2x + 1} = \frac{2}{3}$

4.

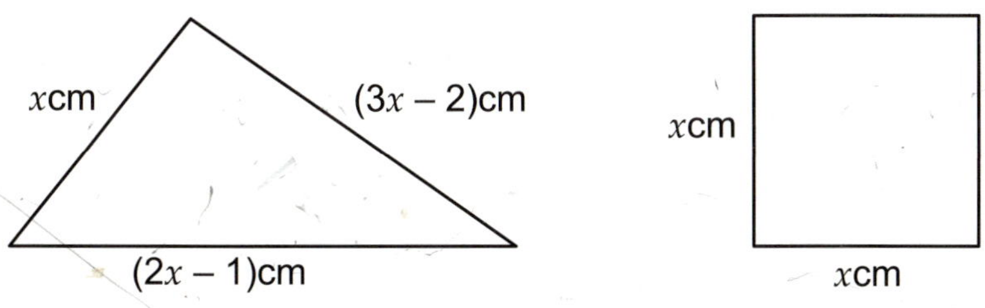

The perimeter of the triangle and the perimeter of the square are equal.
Work out the value of x.

Draw & interpret straight line graphs

When two quantities x and y are connected by an equation such as $y = 3x + 2$ we say that y is a function of x.

A linear function has the form $y = mx + c$
It is called a linear function because it describes a straight line graph.
E.g. $y = 2x + 1$

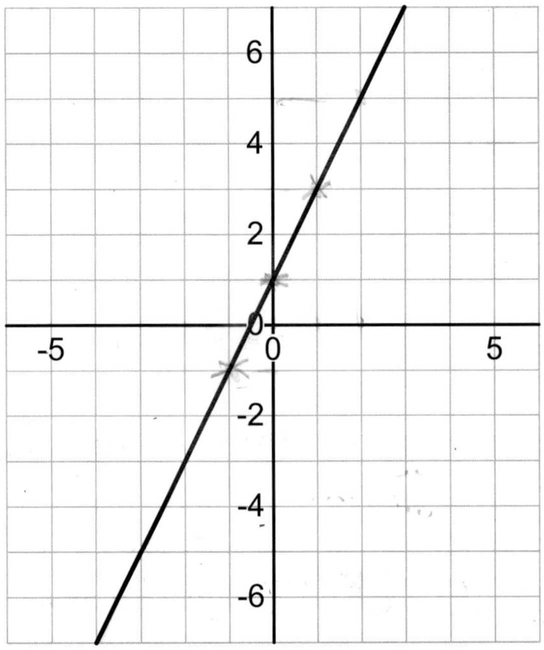

To draw a graph, first make a table. Choose some easy values for x and then find y.

x	−1	0	1
$y = 2x + 1$	−1	1	3

(−1,1) (0,1) (1,3)

The line we draw passes through all 3 points and is extended beyond them.

The number (m) in front of the x tells us the slope or **gradient** of the graph.
For $y = 2x + 1$ the graph goes up 2 squares for every 1 square along. It has gradient 2.

The constant ($+ c$) tells us the **intercept** ~ where the line cuts the y (vertical) axis.

$y = 2x + 1$ intercepts the y axis at 1.

Example

This diagram shows a triangle on a square grid.

The points A, B and C are vertices of the triangle.

Match the correct line to the equation.

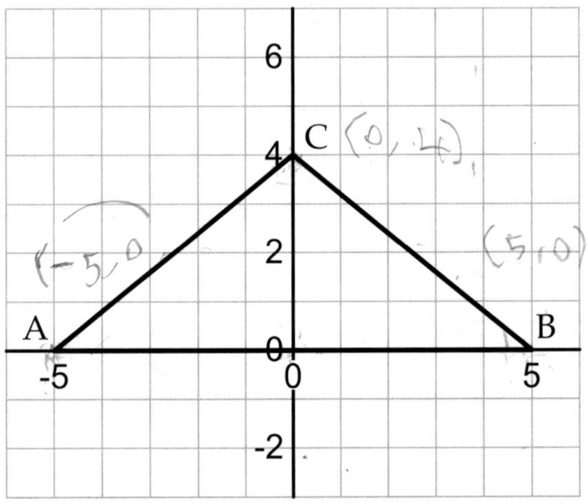

$x = 0$

Line through A and B ⟷ $y = 0$

Line through A and C ⟷ $y = \frac{4}{5}x + 4$

Line through B and C ⟷ $y = \frac{-4}{5}x + 4$

Draw & interpret straight line graphs ~ Questions

1. For each of the following equations:

a) Draw a set of coordinate axes for values of x from –5 to +5.

b) Calculate 3 points on the line $y = x + 2$.

c) Plot your points and draw the line.

i) $y = x + 1$ ii) $y = 2x + 3$ iii) $y = \frac{x}{3} + 3$

iv) $y = 2 - x$ v) $x + y = 4$

2. The diagram shows the graph of a straight line.

a) Write down the gradient of the line.

b) Write down the intercept.

c) Write down the equation of the line.

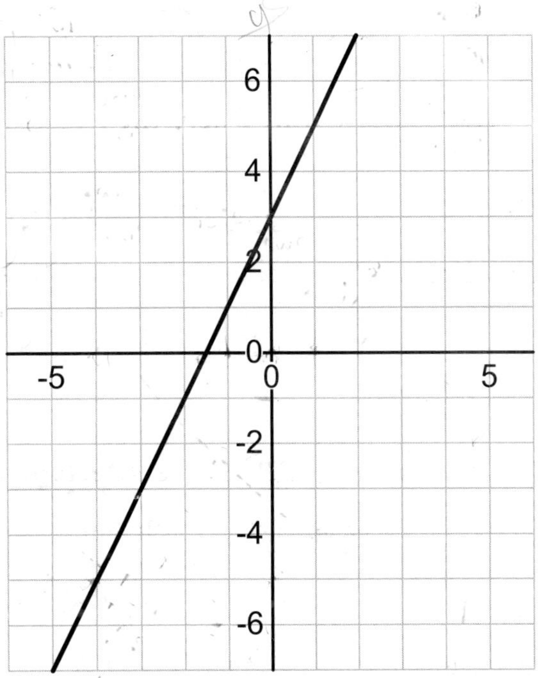

3. The diagram shows a pentagon drawn on a square grid.

Write down an equation for:

a) side AB b) side BC

c) side CD d) side DE

e) side AE

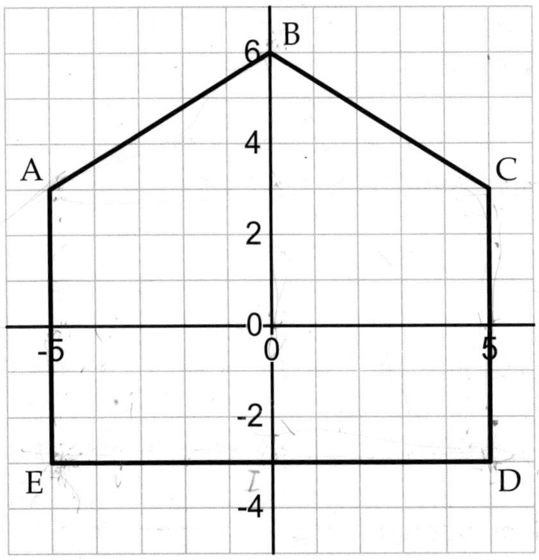

Hockey scores

The hockey match between Shadwell and Humberstone finished with a final score of 3–3.

Jenny and Peter did not watch the game but they saw the final score of 3–3.

1. **When a hockey match finishes with a score of 3-3, show that there could have been 16 different possible half-time scores.**

2. **How many different possible half-time scores could there be for a hockey match with a final score of:**

   a) 0-0 b) 2-1 c) 2-2 d) 4-0 e) 1-3 f) 4-2

3. **Investigate the number of possible half-time scores for a hockey match that finishes with the final scores:**

   a) level b) where one team wins the match

Stacking

Fatima is helping her mother in their shop.
She is stacking some tins on the shelves.

She uses a particular pattern to stack the tins.

Here are two examples of the pattern she uses.

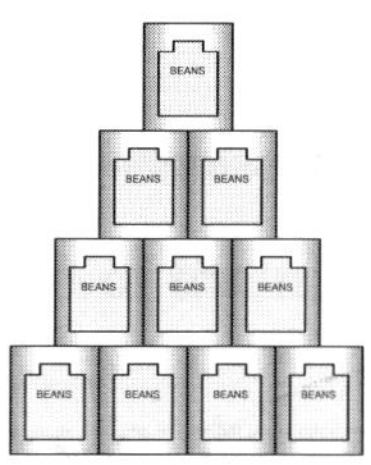

Stage 4
10 tins

Stage 7
28 tins

1. a) Draw stages 5 and 6 of the pattern.

   b) Count the number of tins in stages 5 and 6.

2. Copy and complete this table:

Stage	1	2	3	4	5	6	7	8	9	10
Number of tins				10			28			

3. a) Add together:
   i) The number of tins in stage 4 + the number of tins in stage 5.
   ii) The number of tins in stage 6 + the number of tins in stage 7.
   iii) The number of tins in stage 9 + the number of tins in stage 10.

   b) Write down anything that you notice about the results to part a).

Shapes and symmetry

Here is a square, with its lines of symmetry drawn.

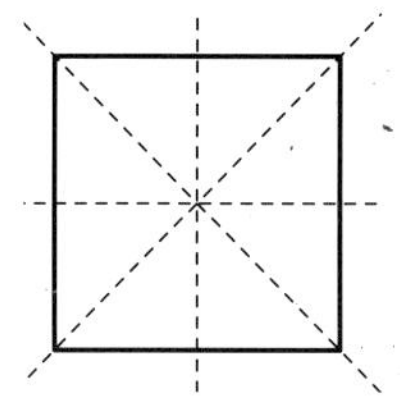

It has: **4 equal sides, 4 right angles,**
4 lines of symmetry and it is two dimensional.

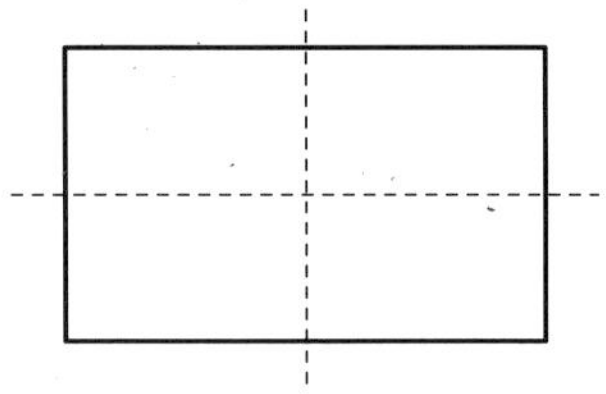

Here is a rectangle, with its lines of symmetry drawn.
It has: **4 sides, 4 right angles** and **2 lines of symmetry** and it is also two dimensional.

Here is a right-angled triangle drawn on a squared grid.
It has: **3 unequal sides, 1 right angle** and **0 lines of symmetry**.

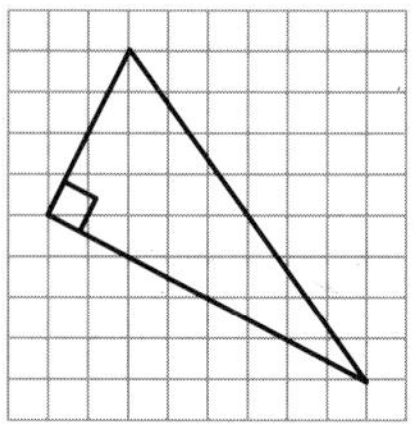

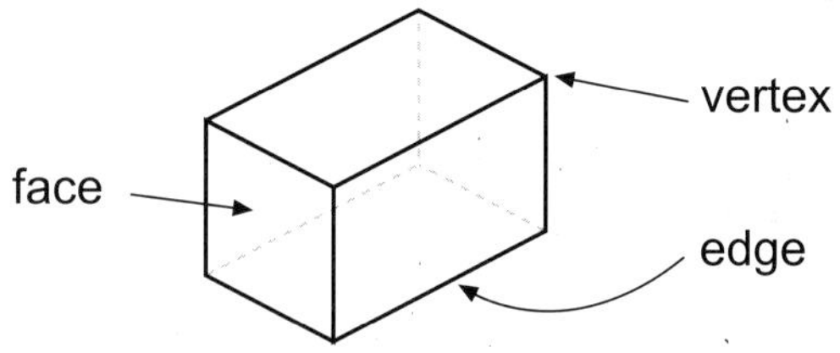

Here is a cuboid. It is three dimensional.
It also has: **6 faces, 8 vertices** and **12 edges.**

An **edge** is the line where **two faces** meet.
A **vertex** is the point where **three (or more) faces** meet.
Each **face** of a cuboid is a **rectangle**.

A **prism** is a 3D shape whose cross-section is constant wherever it is cut.

Here is a:

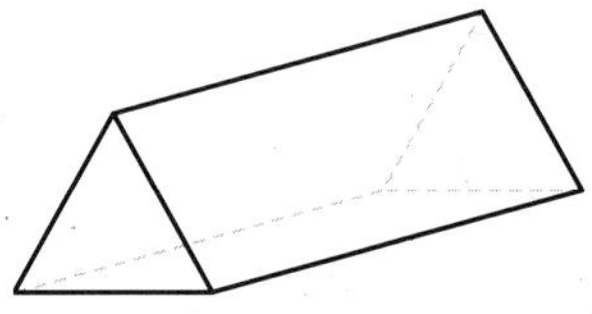

Triangular prism

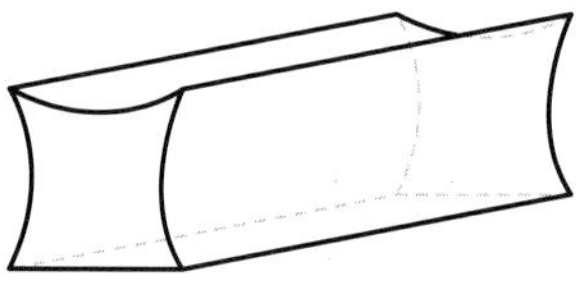

A prism

Here is an L-shape. 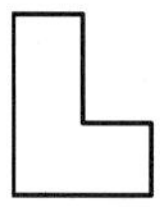

It can be reflected in a line like this: 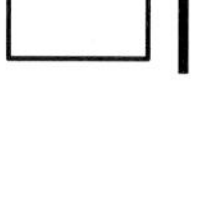 To give us this image: 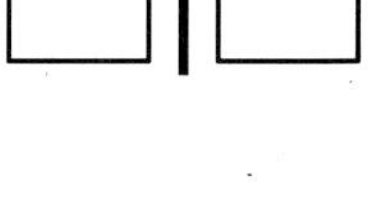

Shapes and symmetry ~ Questions

1. **Draw each shape.**
   a) Equilateral triangle
   b) Isosceles triangle
   c) Parallelogram
   d) Rhombus
   e) Square
   f) Trapezium
   g) Kite
   h) Rectangle

2. **Copy these shapes and draw all the lines of symmetry.**

   a) 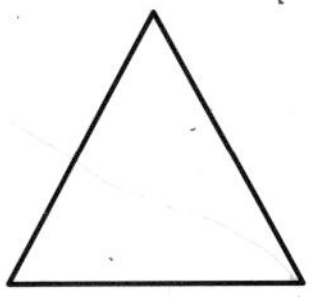
   b) 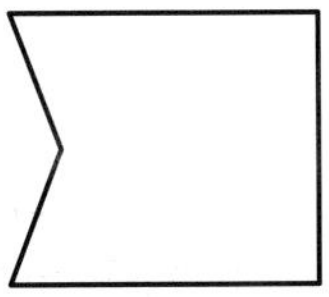
   c) 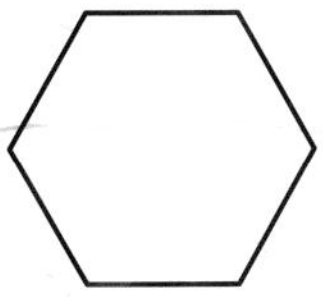
   d) 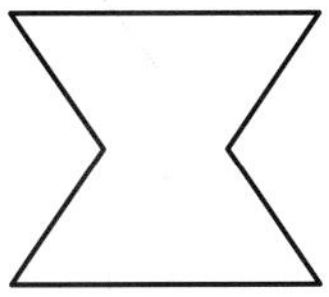

3. **Draw a two dimensional shape which has:**
   a) 4 sides and 4 lines of symmetry
   b) 3 sides and 1 line of symmetry
   c) 8 sides and 8 lines of symmetry
   d) 4 sides and 0 lines of symmetry

4. **Draw on graph paper:**
   a) A square
   b) A rectangle
   c) A right angled, isosceles triangle

5. **List as many 3D shapes as you can in this picture.**

6. **State the number of: i) faces ii) edges iii) vertices on:**

   a) 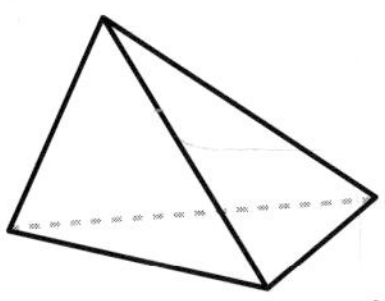
   b) 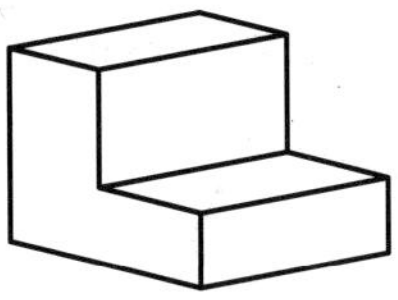

7. **Reflect each 2D shape in the line.**

   a) 
   b) 
   c) 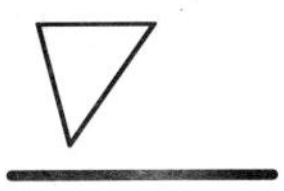
   d) 
   e) 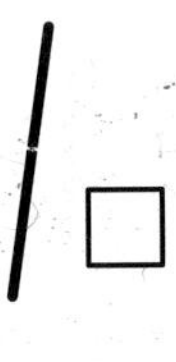
   f) 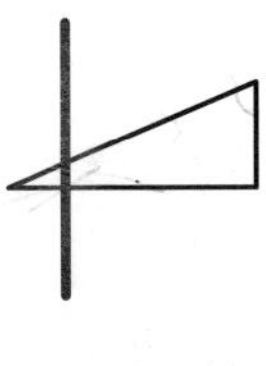

Co-ordinates

Here is a grid, it is called a **co-ordinate grid**.

Various points are labelled for you.

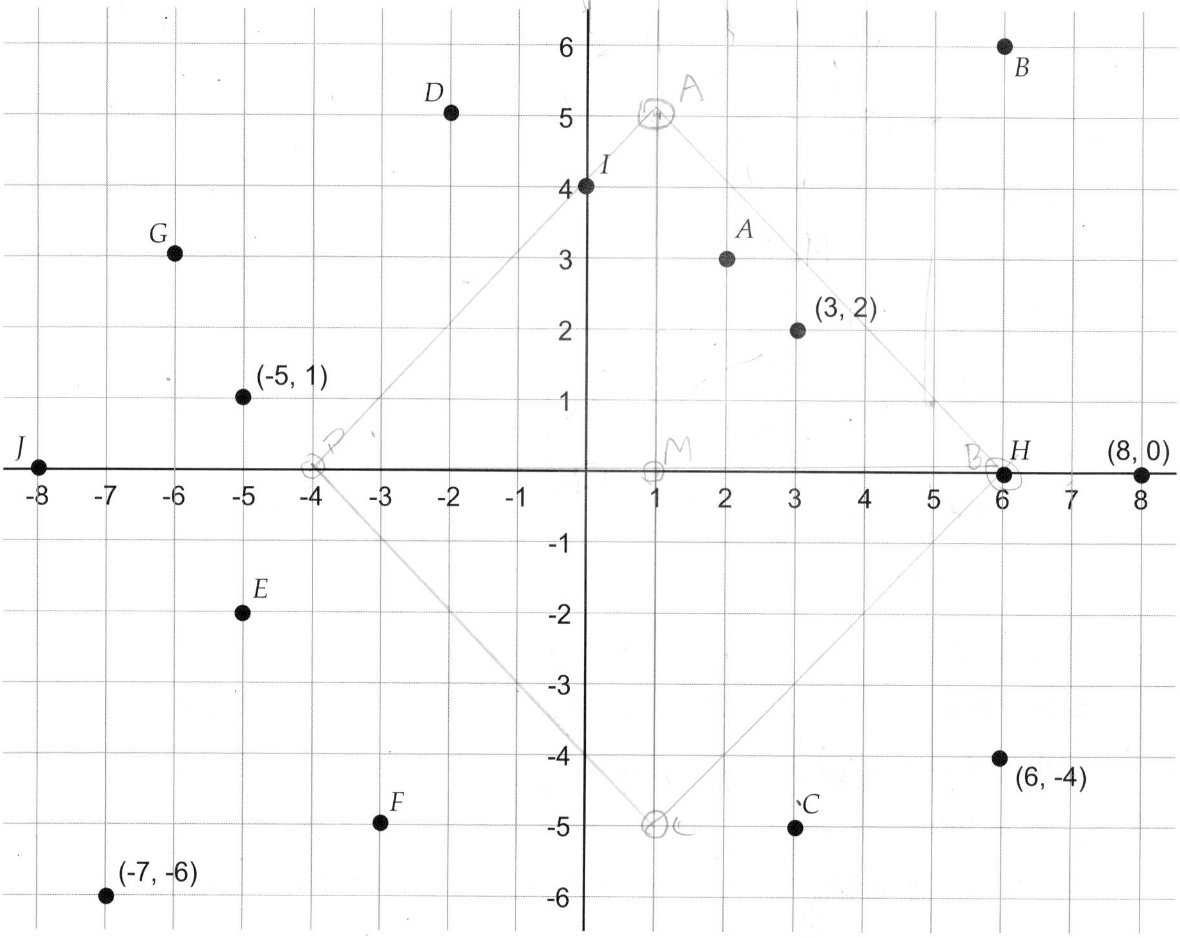

Start at the origin (**0**, **0**) then move **3 to the right** and **2 up** gets us to (**3**, **2**).

Start at the origin (**0**, **0**) then move **5 to the left** and **1 up** gets us to (**–5**, **1**).

Start at the origin (**0**, **0**) then move **7 to the left** and **6 down** gets us to (**–7**, **–6**).

Start at the origin (**0**, **0**) then move **6 to the right** and **4 down** gets us to (**6**, **–4**).

Start at the origin (**0**, **0**) then move **8 to the right** but **none up or down** gets us to (**8**, **0**).

Shape and space 1

Co-ordinates ~ Questions

1. a) Look at the co-ordinate grid across the page and write down the co-ordinates of all of the points: *A, B, C, D, E, F, G, H, I* and *J*.

b) Using a ruler, measure the distance from (0, 0) to the point with co-ordinates (6, –4).

2. On a fresh grid:

a) Plot the points: *A* (1, 1), *B* (5, 1), *C* (5, 5) and *D* (1, 5).

b) Draw the shape *ABCD*.

c) Name the shape *ABCD*.

d) Work out the area of the shape *ABCD*.

e) Work out the co-ordinates of the point *M*, the centre of the shape *ABCD*.

3. On a fresh grid:

a) Draw the line segment *PQ* that goes from the points *P* (1, 2) to *Q* (7, 8).

b) Find the co-ordinates of the mid-point of the line segment.

4. On a fresh grid:

a) Plot the points with co-ordinates: *A* (1, 5), *B* (6, 0), *C* (1, –5) and D (–4, 0).

b) Join the points *A* to *B*, *B* to *C*, *C* to *D* and *D* to *A*.

c) Name the shape *ABCD*.

d) Work out the co-ordinates of the point *M*, which is at the centre of the shape *ABCD*.

5. ***PQRS*** **is a rectangle.**

The point *S* is not shown.

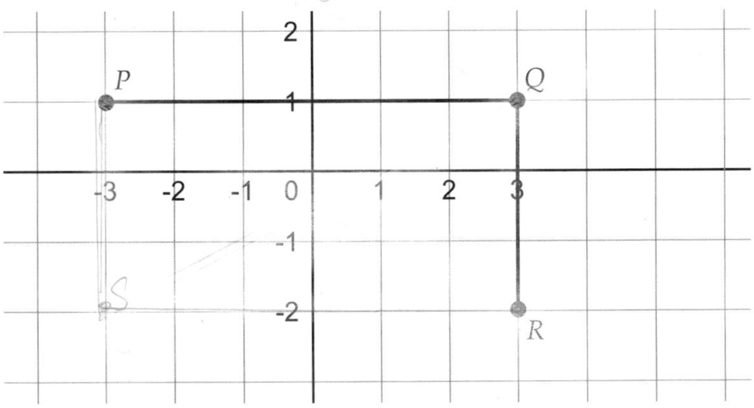

a) Find the co-ordinates of the point *S*.

b) Work out the area of *PQRS*.

c) Draw the lines *PR* and *QS*.

d) Write down the co-ordinates of the point where the two lines cross.

Quadrilaterals

A quadrilateral has 4 sides.

A square	4 equal sides. Opposite sides are parallel and 4 equal angles of 90°. Rotational symmetry of order 4. 4 lines of symmetry.	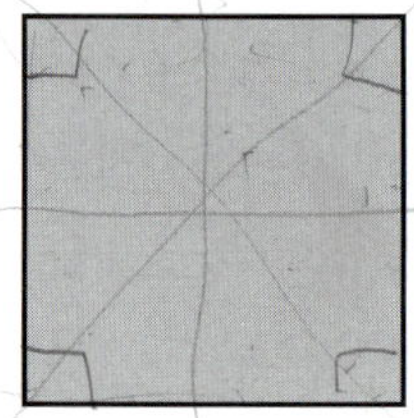
A rectangle	4 equal sides. Opposite sides are parallel and 4 equal angles of 90°. Rotational symmetry of order 2. 2 lines of symmetry.	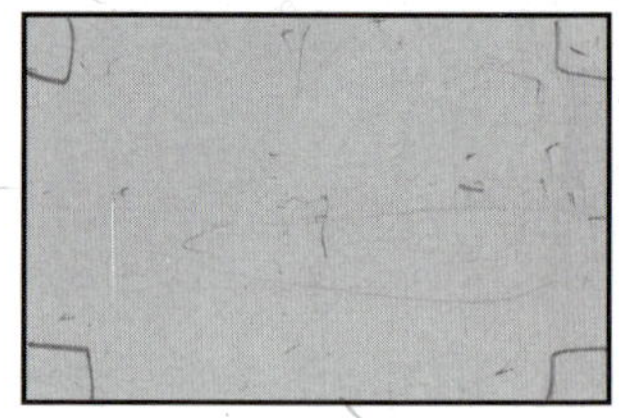
A parallelogram	Opposite sides are equal. Opposite sides are parallel and opposite angles are equal. Rotational symmetry of order 2. No lines of symmetry.	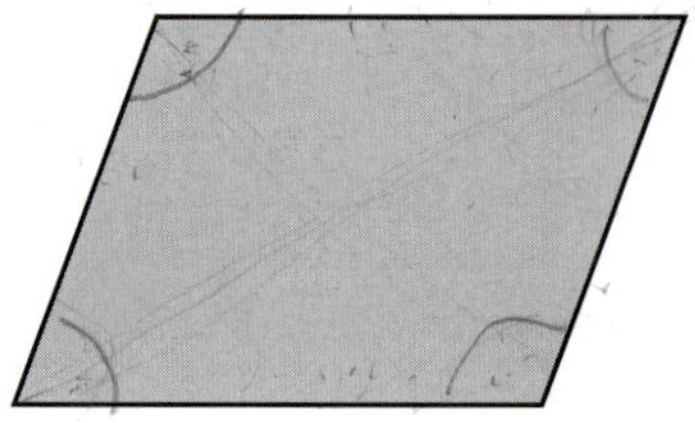
A rhombus	4 equal sides. Opposite sides are parallel and opposite angles are equal. Rotational symmetry of order 2. 2 lines of symmetry.	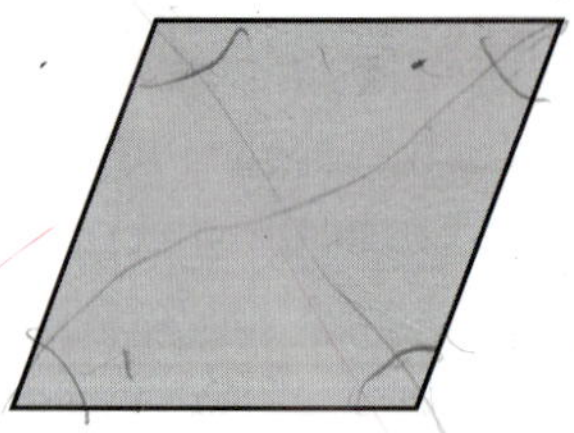
A trapezium	1 pair of parallel sides. Some trapeziums have a line of symmetry.	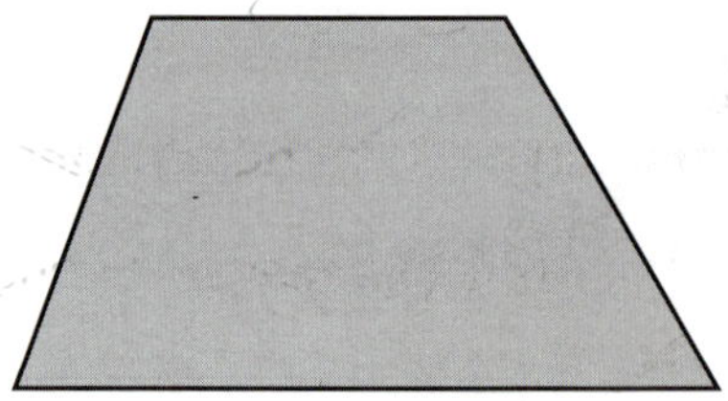
A kite	Adjacent sides are equal. 1 pair of opposite angles are equal. 1 line of symmetry.	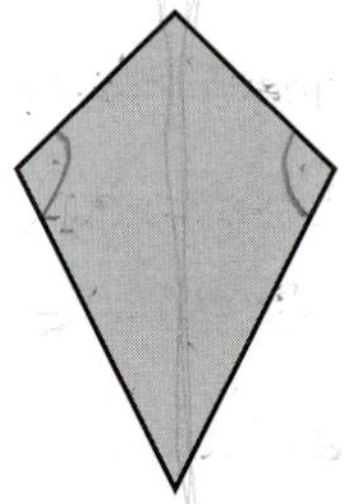

Quadrilaterals ~ Questions

1. **Draw a set of co-ordinate axes as shown.**

   Plot each set of points and join them up in order to form a quadrilateral.

   a) Name the quadrilateral.

   b) Mark any lines of symmetry on your diagram.

   c) Write down the order rotational symmetry.

   d) Mark the angles which are equal and label the parallel lines.

   i) $A(2,5)$ $B(7,3)$ $C(7,7)$ $D(9,5)$

   ii) $A(2,1)$ $B(2,5)$ $C(6,5)$ $D(6,1)$

   iii) $A(2,6)$ $B(4,6)$ $C(6,3)$ $D(2,3)$

   iv) $A(2,4)$ $B(5,5)$ $C(8,4)$ $D(5,3)$

   v) $A(3,4)$ $B(8,6)$ $C(7,3)$ $D(2,1)$

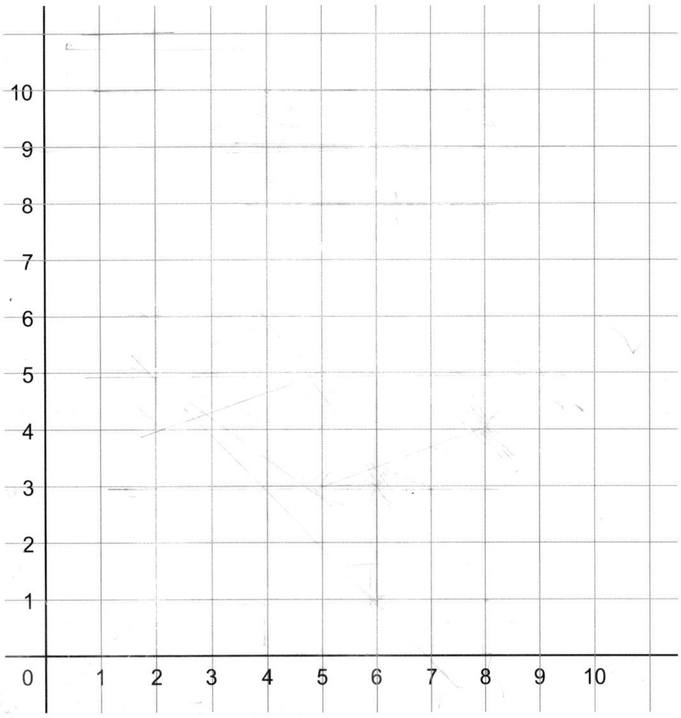

2. **Name the quadrilateral:**

   a) This quadrilateral has one pair of parallel sides and no lines of symmetry.

   b) This quadrilateral has 1 line of symmetry but has no parallel sides.

3. **Ahmed says, "This quadrilateral has 4 equal sides, so it must be a square."**

   Explain why he may be wrong.

4. **Jane says, "This quadrilateral has 2 pairs of equal sides, so it must be a rectangle."**

   Explain why she may be wrong.

5. **Explain how:**

   a) a rectangle could be a square.

   b) a rhombus could be a parallelogram.

   c) a square could be a parallelogram.

   In each case say what happens to the lines of symmetry.

Measures

Their teacher asked Joseph and Isabel to measure the width of their desk using **hand spans.**

Joseph measured his and got an answer of **3 hand spans.**

Isabel measured hers and got an answer of **3 and a half hand spans.**

The desks were the same length, but their results were different because a **hand span** is not a **standard unit** of length. Two people can have hand spans of different length.

When Joseph and Isabel measured the width of their desk using a ruler, they both found it to be exactly 60 centimetres, a centimetre is a **standard unit** of length.

Here is a list of some **standard metric** units of length, capacity and mass:

Length	Capacity	Mass
1 millimetre (mm)	1 millilitre (ml)	1 milligram (mg)
1 centimetre (1cm = 10mm)	1 centilitre (1cl = 10ml)	1 gram (1g = 1000mg)
1 metre (1m = 100cm)	1 litre (1l = 100cl)	1 kilogram (1kg = 1000g)
1 kilometre (1km = 100m)	1 tonne (1t = 1000kg)	

Reading scales

The division marks on scales do not always go up by 1 at a time. Some go up by 2, others by 5 or even by 10 or more units.

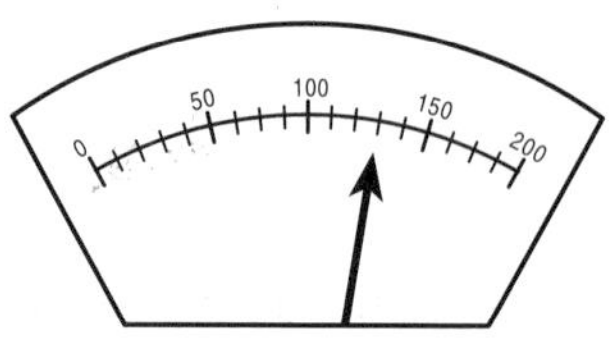

Each division shows **10g**.

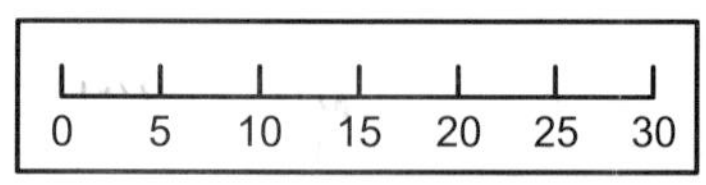

Whist this one shows **5kg** per division.

Time

Here are three clock faces. Each one shows a time of exactly 9 o'clock.

This shows **9 o'clock** in the morning (**am**) or **9 o'clock** in the evening (pm).

This shows **9 o'clock** in the morning (**am**).

This shows **9 o'clock** in the evening (**pm**).

NB: am means anti-meridian, pm means post-meridian.

Measures ~ Questions

1. **Measure the length of each line.**

   Give each answer in millimetres and centimetres.

   a) ____________ b) ________________________________

   c) ____

2. **Write down the mass of:**

   a) 5 grams in milligrams b) 3 kilograms in grams

3. **Georgie shared 2 litres of milk equally between her four children.**

   Work out each person's share in centilitres.

4. **Write down the time shown on each of these clock faces:**

   a) 

   b) 

   c) 

   d) 

   e) 

   f) 

5. **Draw six clock faces and show:**

   a) four o'clock b) ten past seven c) twenty to three

   d) quarter past six e) twenty-five to ten f) five past eleven

6. **Draw six digital clocks and show each of the following times:**

   a) quarter to ten b) eleven o'clock c) ten past two

   d) three o'clock e) five to eight f) twenty to twelve

7. **Write down the reading on each of these scales:**

   a) 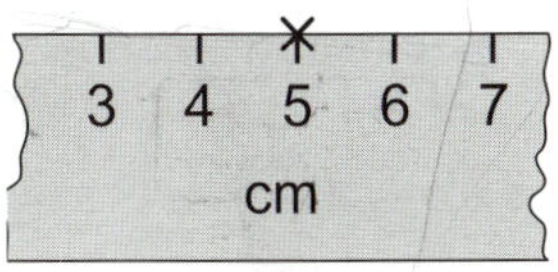

   b) 

   c) 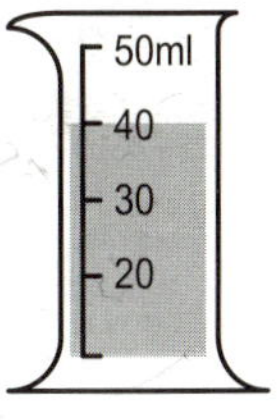

   d) 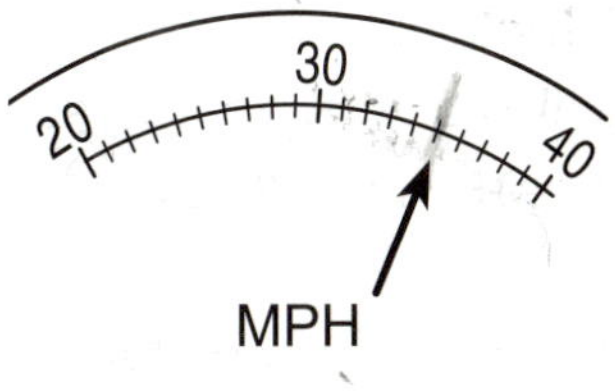

Measuring angles

You need to be able to use an angle measurer to draw and measure angles. There is always a scale drawing question.

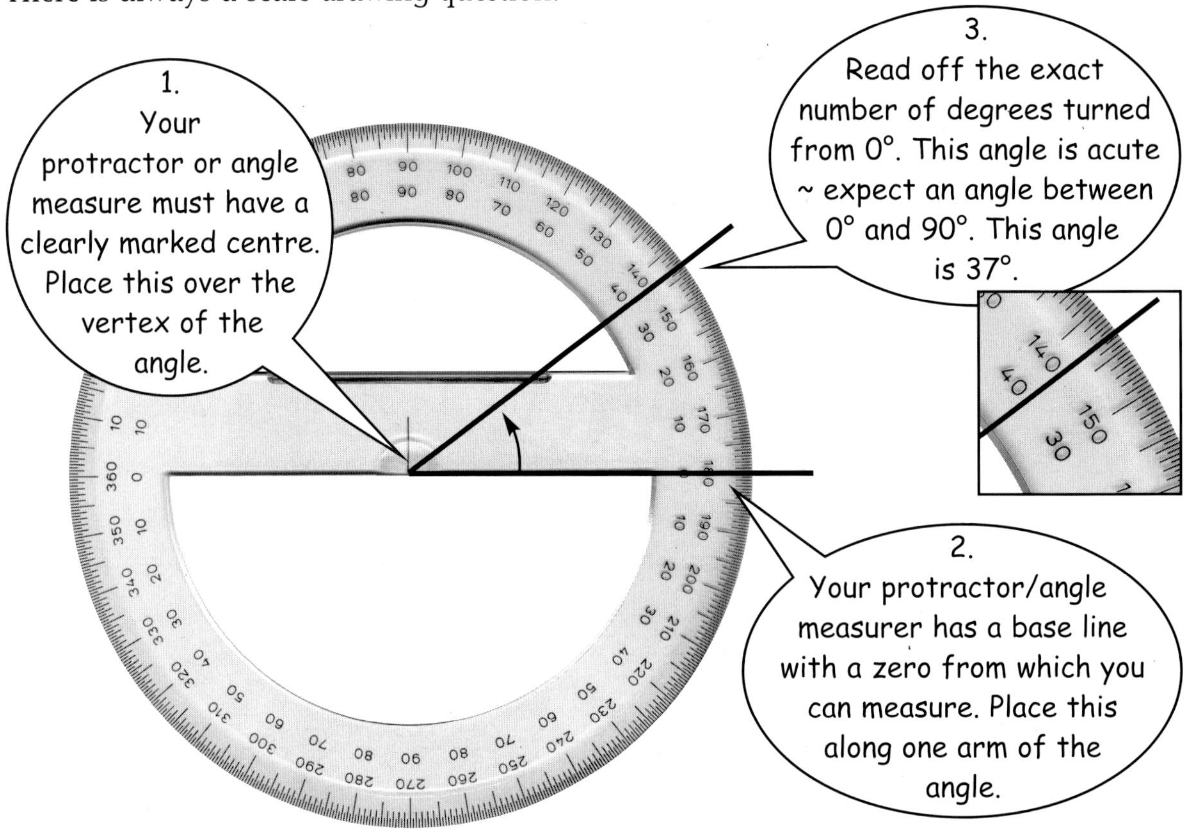

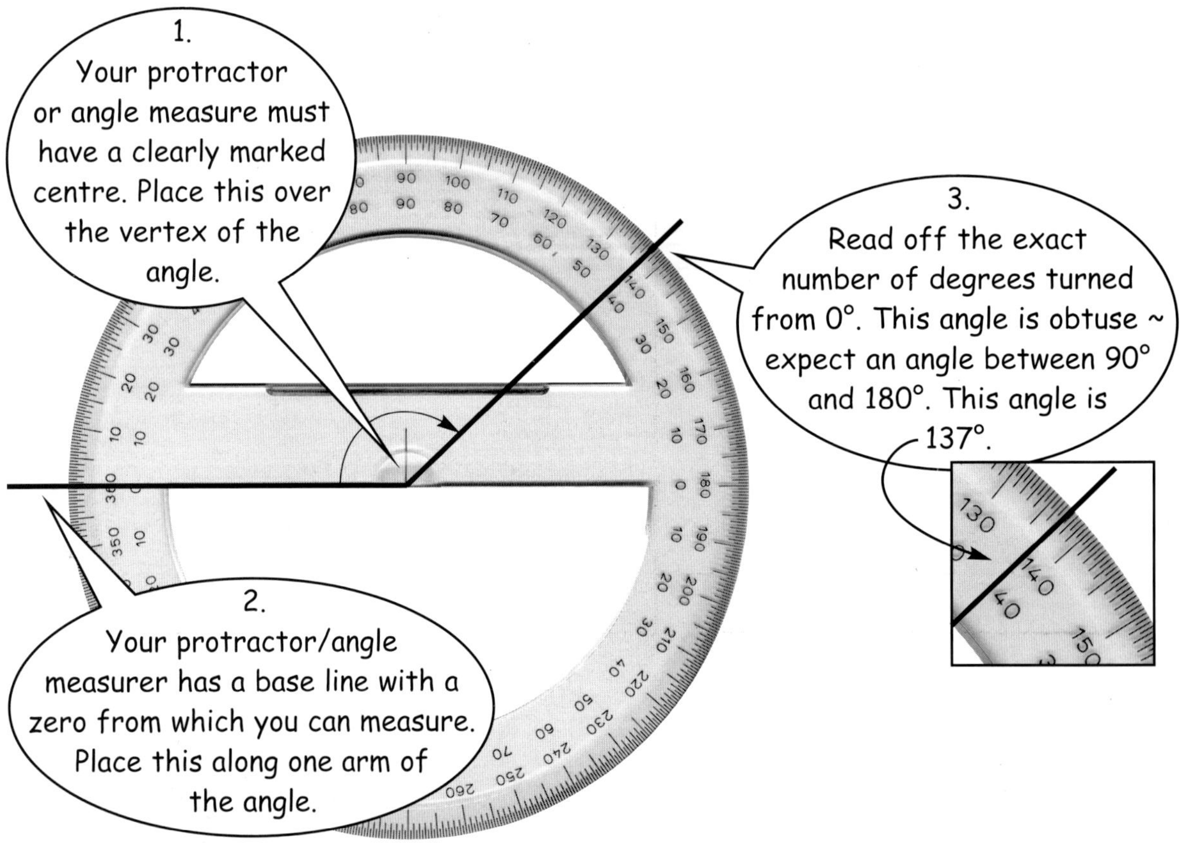

Measuring angles ~ Questions

1. **Measure this angle.**

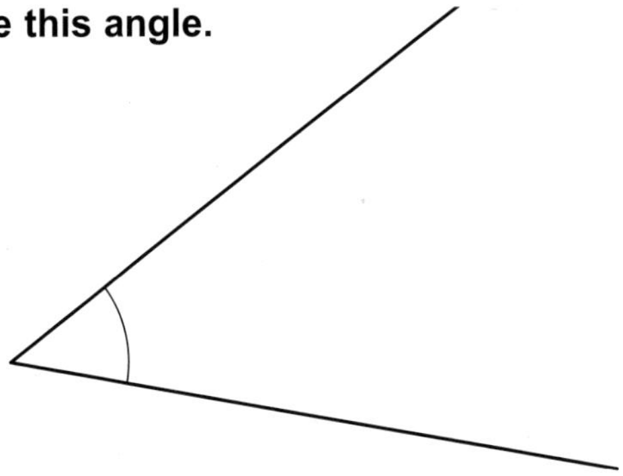

2. **Measure this angle.**

   (it is obtuse.)

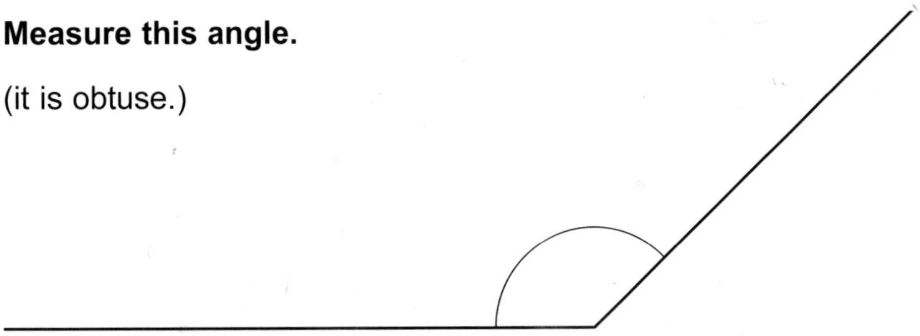

3. **Measure the angles marked with letters.**

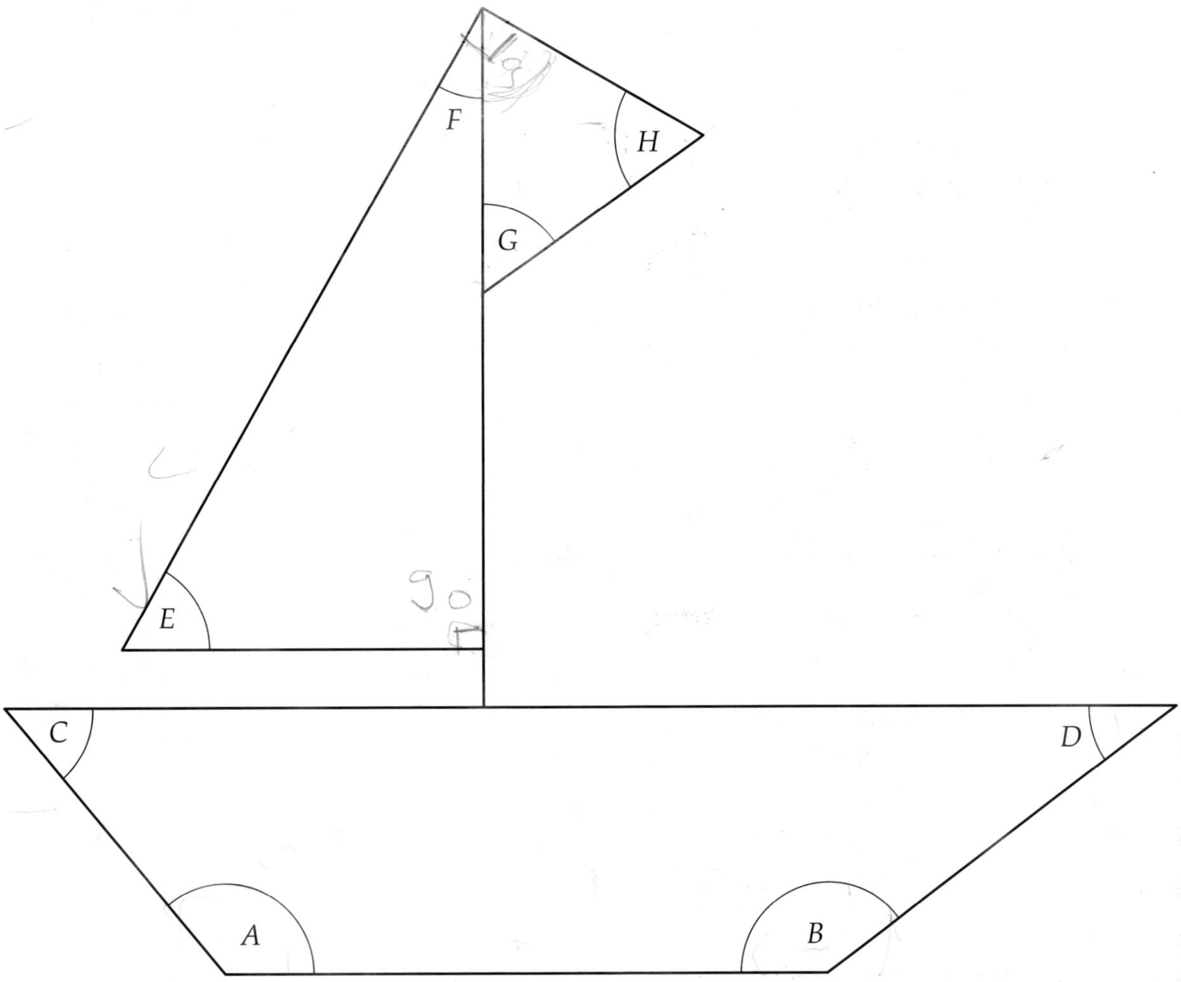

Drawing angles

To draw an angle you must begin with a baseline.
On the SAT test you are usually given a baseline.

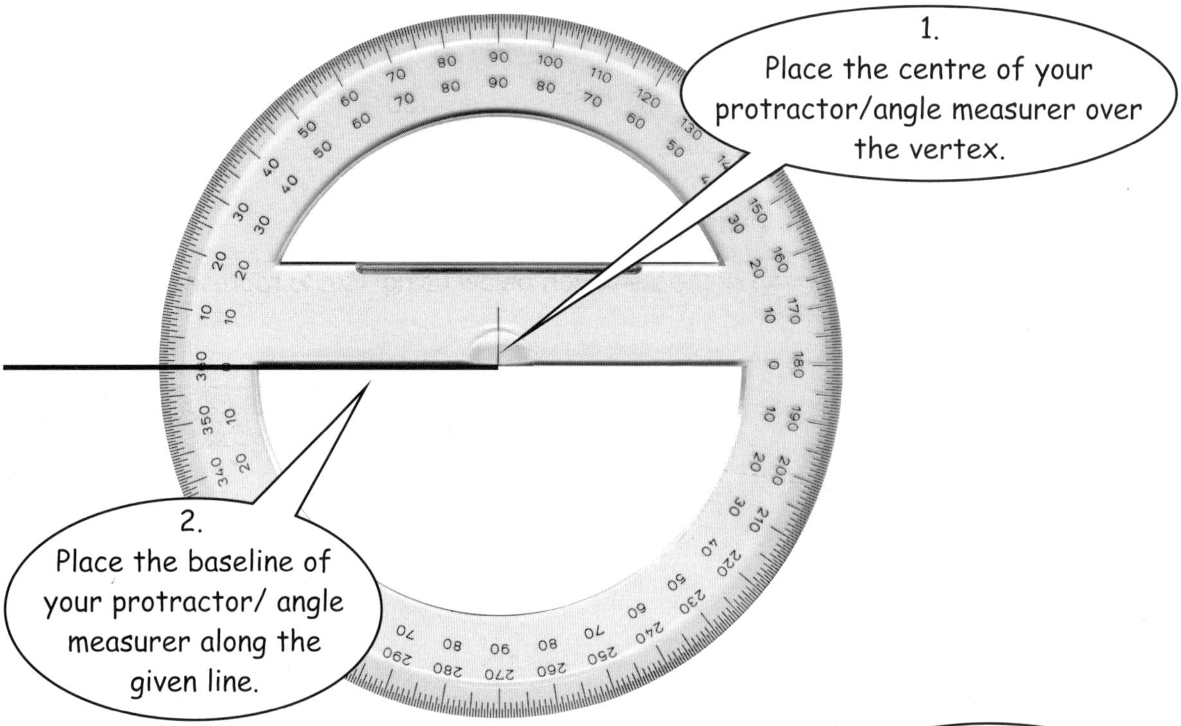

To draw an angle of 120°:

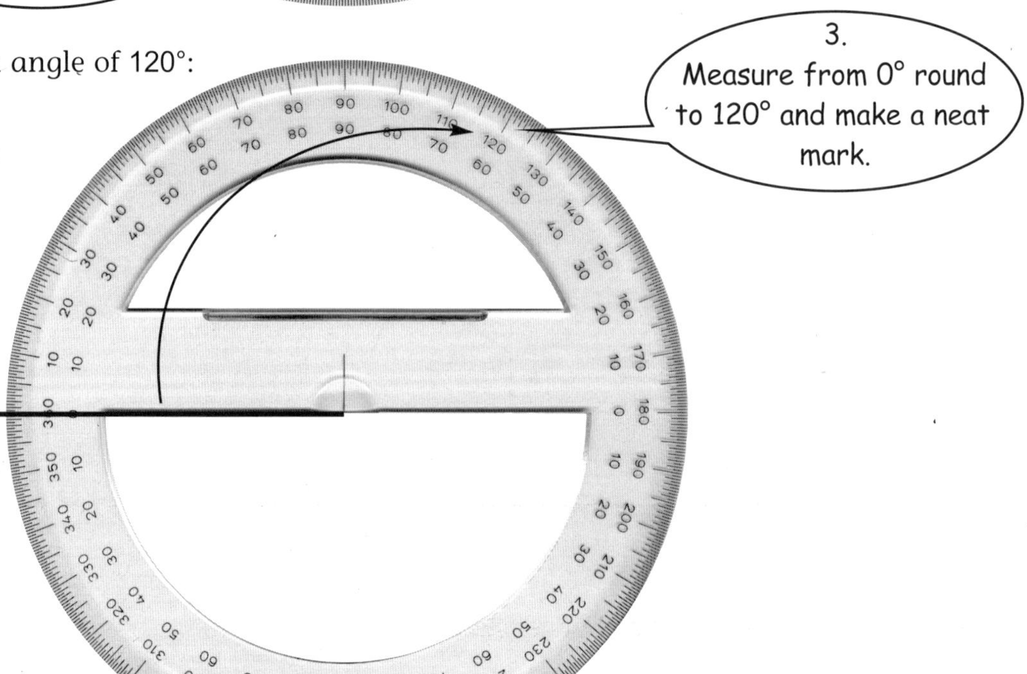

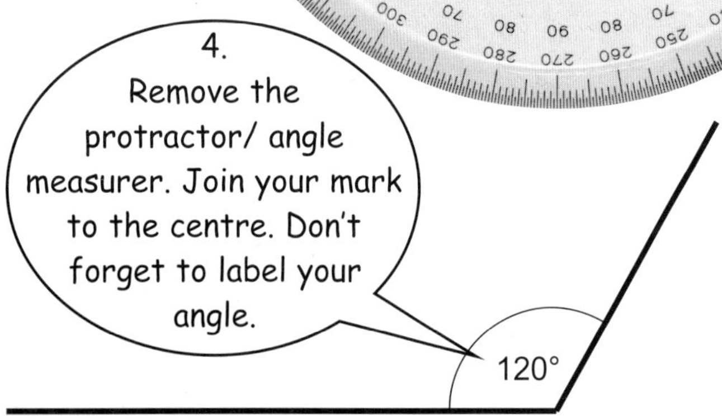

Drawing angles ~ Questions

Make sure you have a sharp pencil!

1. **Draw the following angles:**

   a) 45° b) 73° c) 156° d) 105° e) 195° f) 203°

2. **The diagram is a sketch of a pentagon.**

   Make an accurate scale drawing of the pentagon below using 1cm to represent 1m.

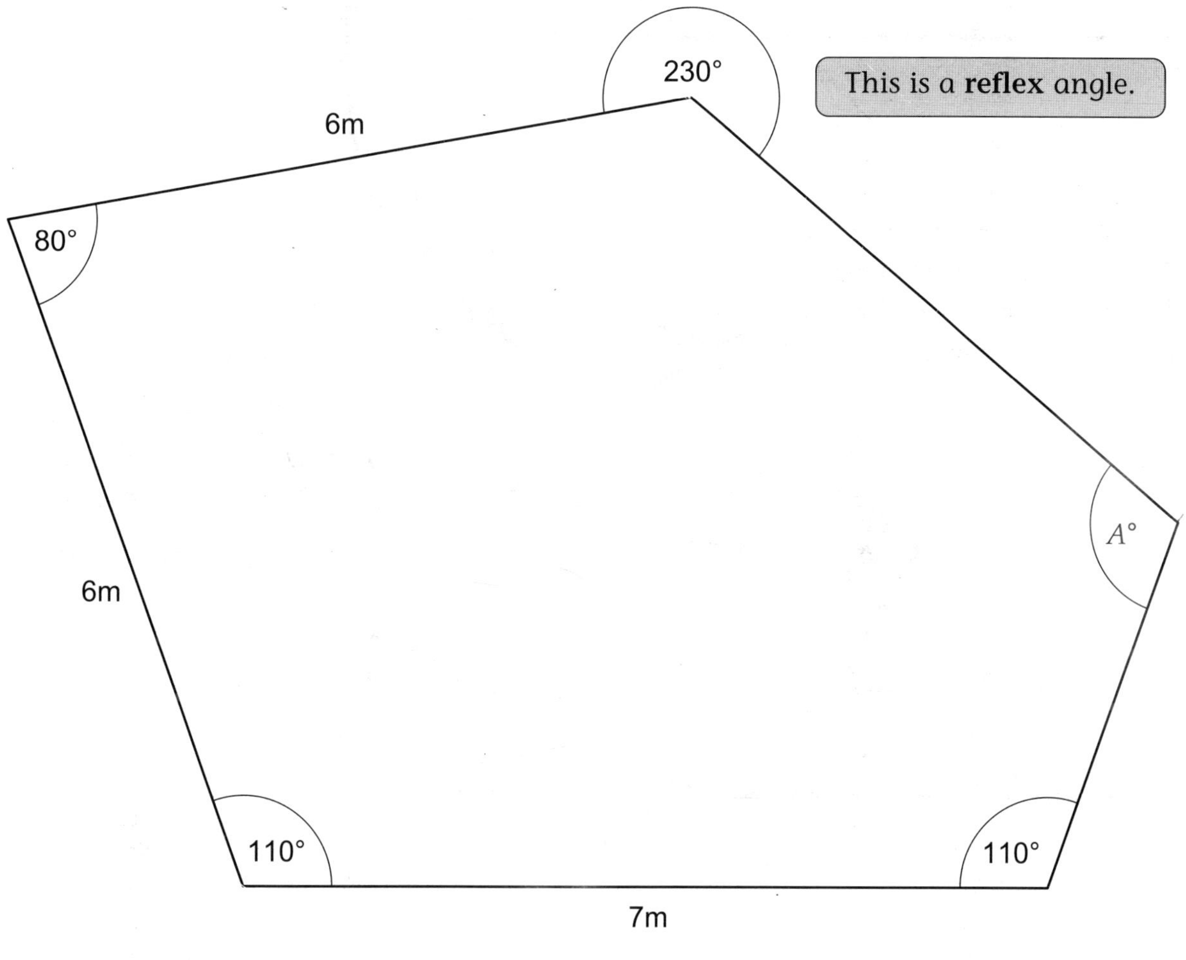

Measure the angle $A°$ and the shortest side.

Sum = (n−2) × 180

Angles

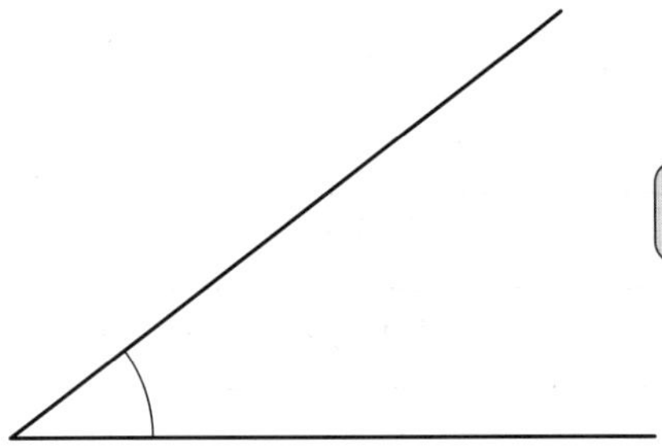

An acute angle is between 0° and 90°.

An obtuse angle is between 90° and 180°.

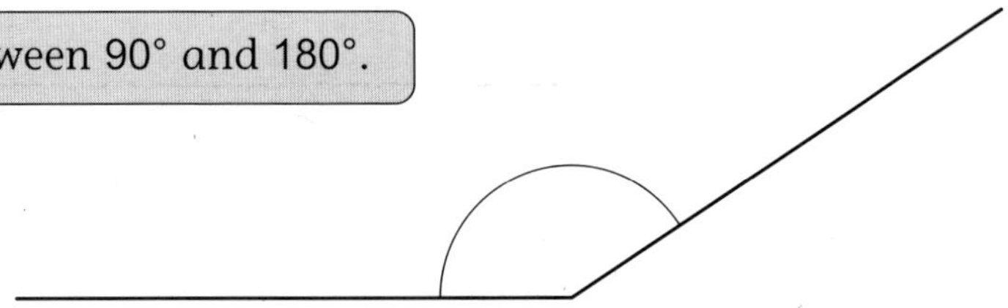

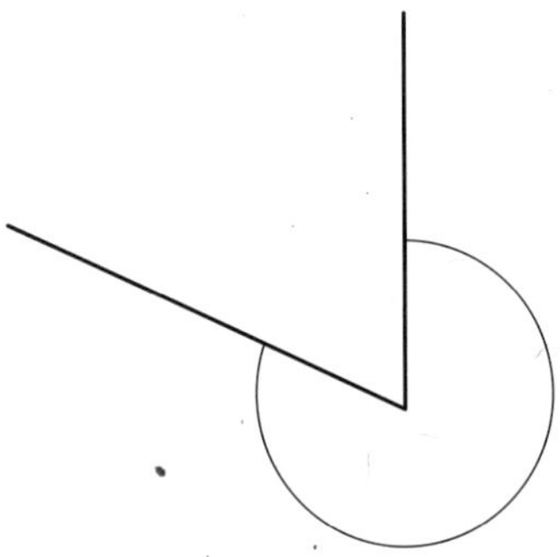

A reflex angle is between 180° and 360°.

Angles on a straight line add up to 180°:
$a° + b° + c° = 180°$

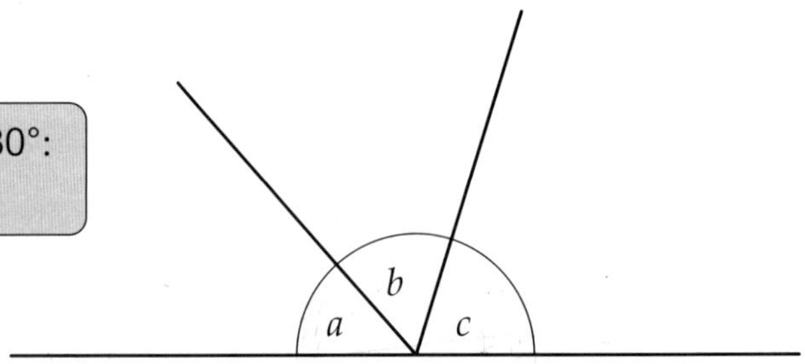

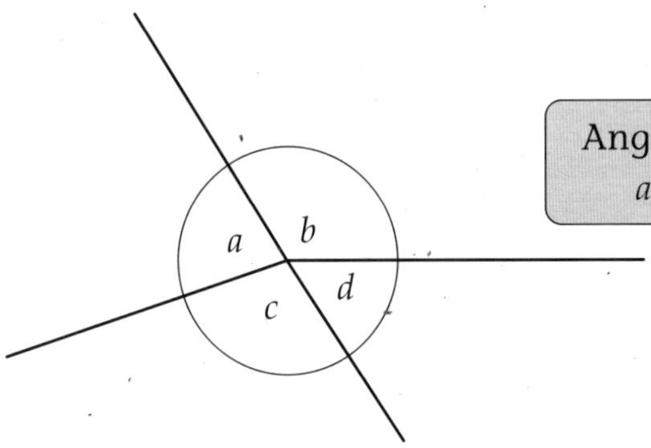

Angles at a point add up to 360°:
$a° + b° + c° + d° = 360°$

When reading or writing angles, the angle is the middle letter.
$<BCA$ or $B\hat{C}A$

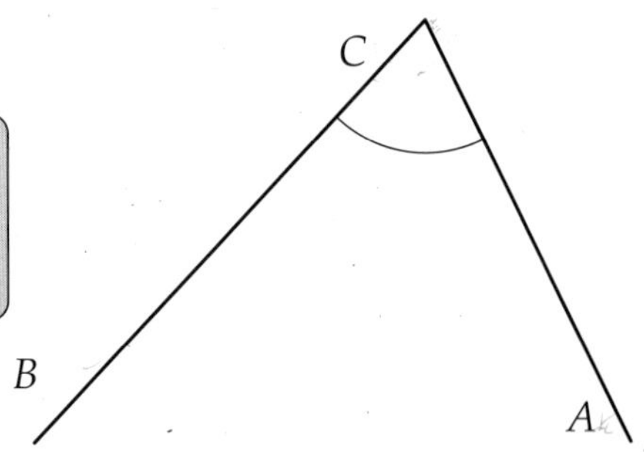

Angles ~ Questions

1. Copy and fill in the table with the correct name for the angle and its type.
The first one has been done for you:

	ANGLE	TYPE
a)	<*ACB*	Obtuse
b)		
c)		
d)		

a)
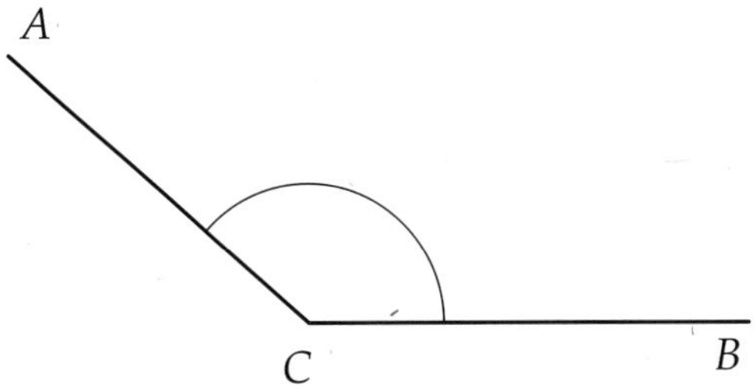

b)
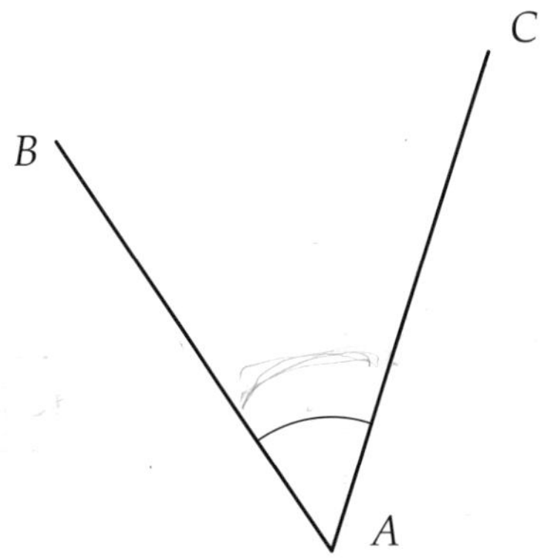

c)
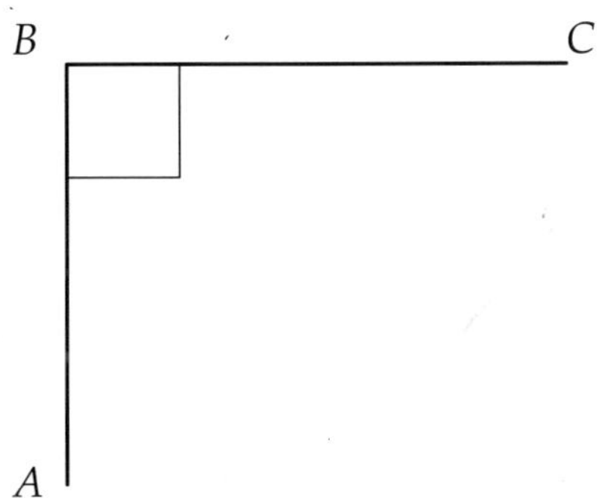

d)
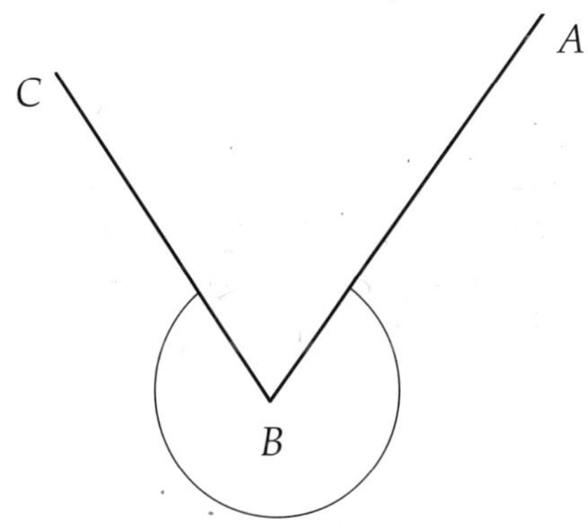

2. Find the missing angles marked with letters:

a)
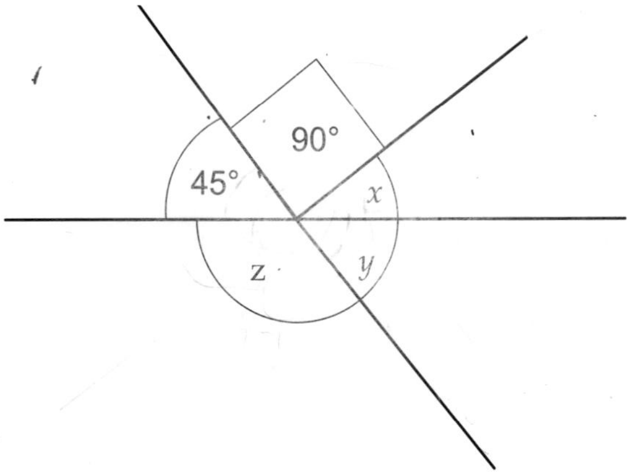

b)
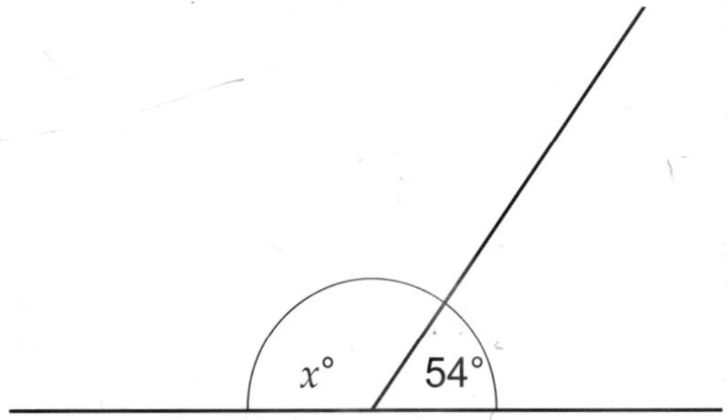

Intersecting and parallel lines

Angles at a point add up to 360°.

$a + b + c + d = 360°$

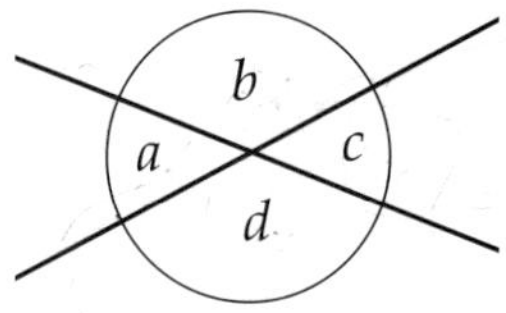

Angles on a straight line add up to 180°.

$a + b + c = 180°$

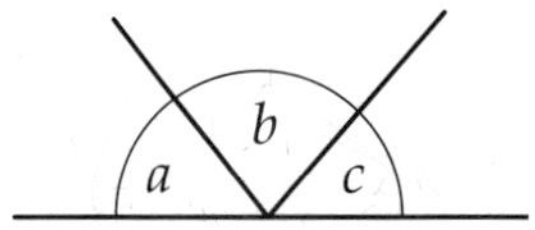

Vertically opposite angles are equal.

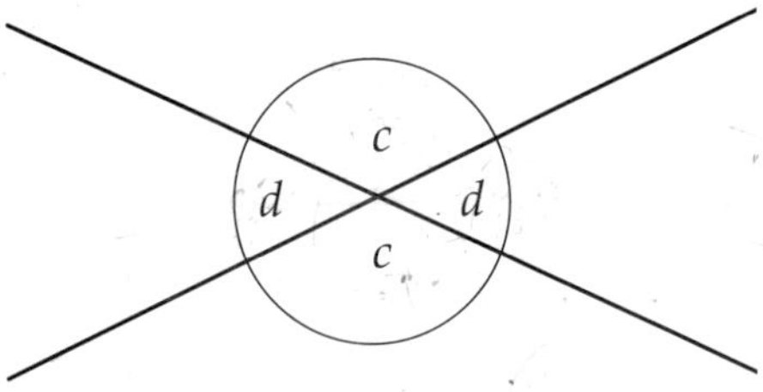

Alternate (z) angles are equal.

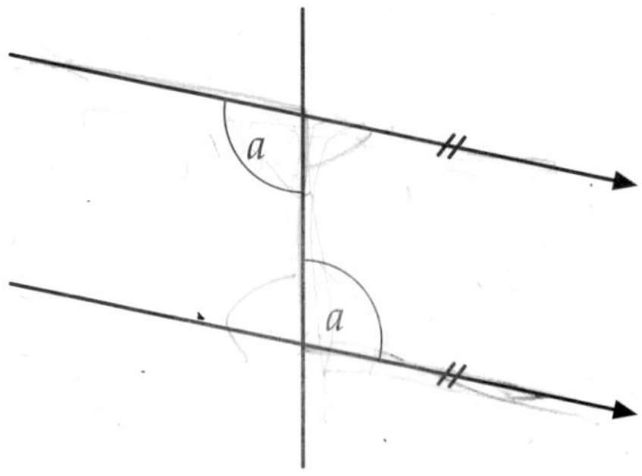

Corresponding angles F are equal.

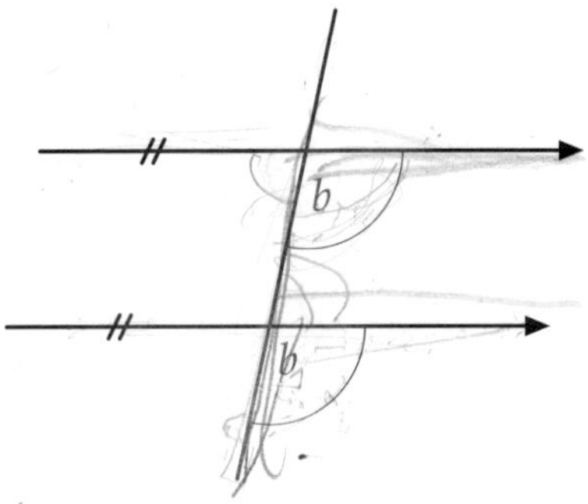

(The horizontal lines are parallel.)

Supplementary angles add up to 180°.

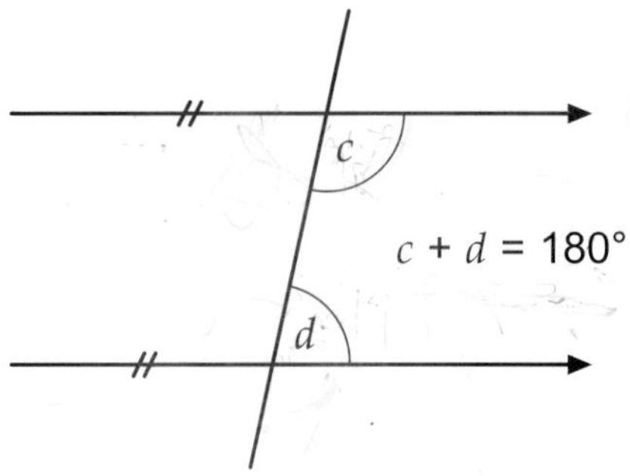

Example:

Find the angles marked with letters and give reasons for your answers.

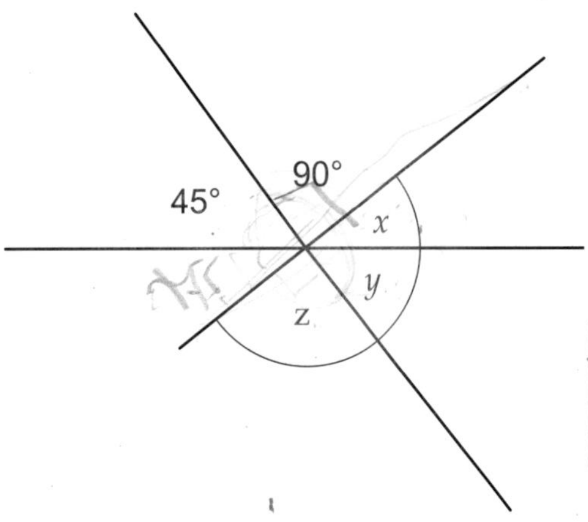

$x = 180° - 90° - 45°$ angles on a straight line
$x = 45°$
$y = 45°$ vertically opposite angles
$z = 90°$ vertically opposite angles

Do not attempt to measure. They will have been deliberately drawn as the wrong size!

Intersecting and parallel lines ~ Questions

1. **Find angle a.**
   Give a reason for your answer.

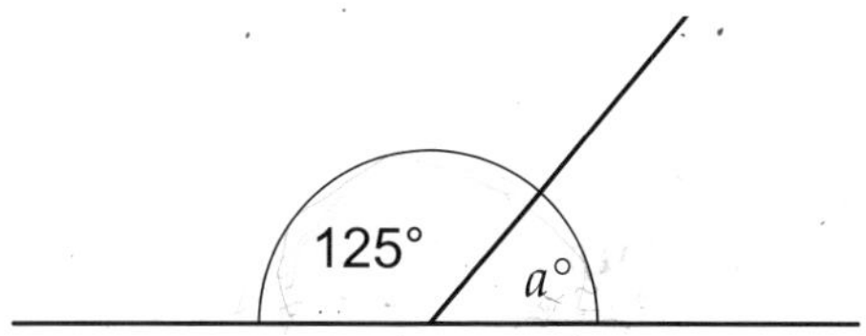

2. **Jane says:**

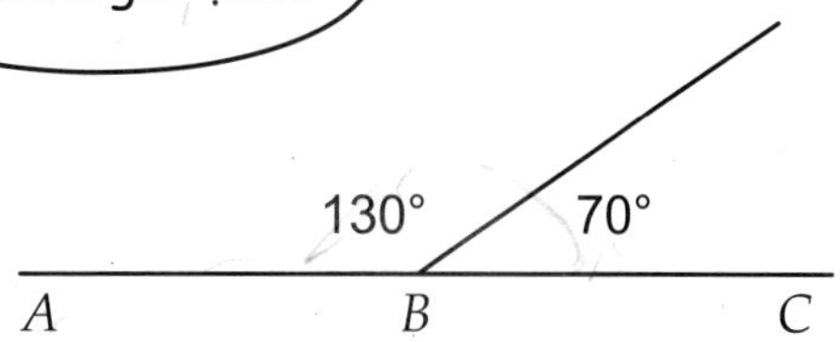

   Explain why she is wrong.

3. **Jack says:**

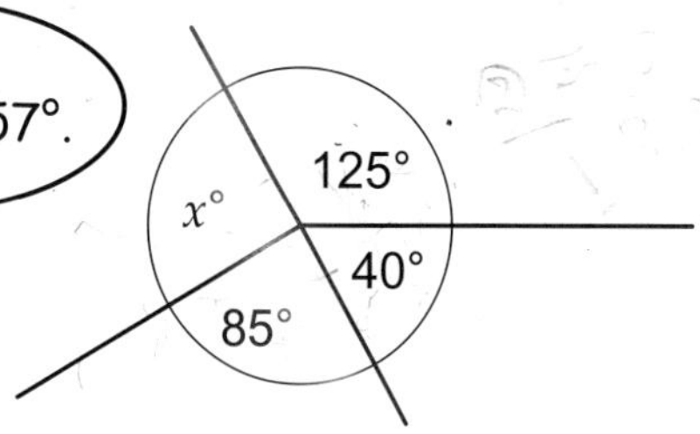

   Explain why he is wrong.

4. **Copy the diagram:**

   a) Label with an X a pair of alternate angles.
   b) Label with a Y pair of corresponding angles.
   c) Label with a Z two angles which add up to 180°.

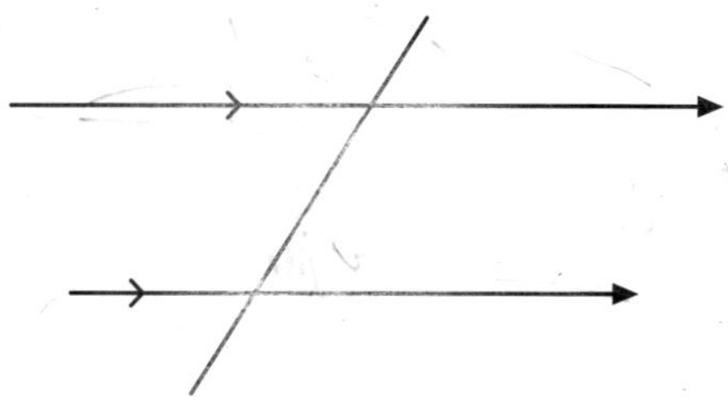

5. **Calculate the angle marked x.**
   Give a reason for your answer.

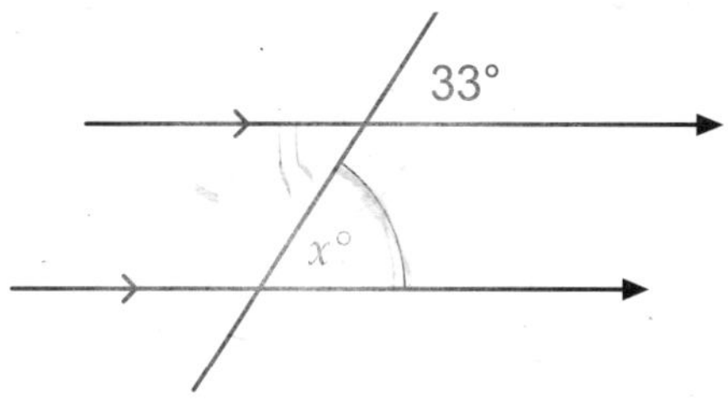

6. **Explain why the lines AB and CD cannot be parallel.**

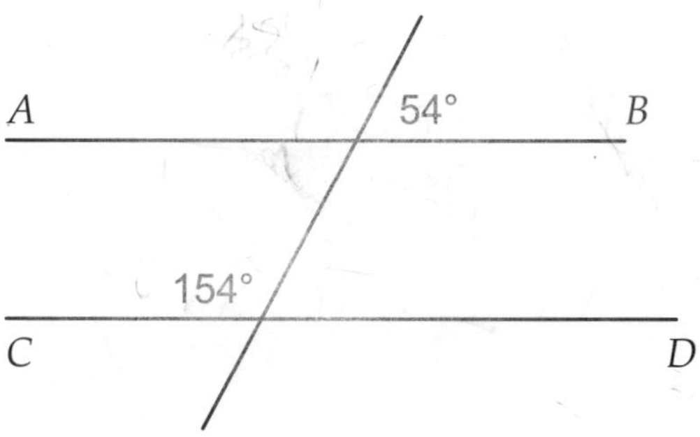

The angles in triangles & quadrilaterals

To prove the interior angles of a triangle add up to 180°:

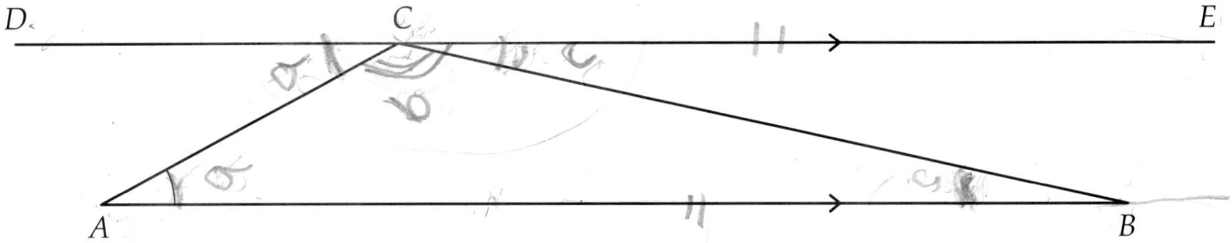

Draw a line through the vertex C parallel to the base of the triangle AB.

$A\hat{C}D + A\hat{C}B + B\hat{C}E = 180°$	angles on a straight line
$A\hat{C}D = B\hat{A}C$	alternate angles
$B\hat{C}E = A\hat{B}C$	alternate angles
$\therefore B\hat{A}C + A\hat{C}B + A\hat{B}C = 180°$	

To prove the exterior angle of a triangle is equal to the sum of the two opposite interior angles:

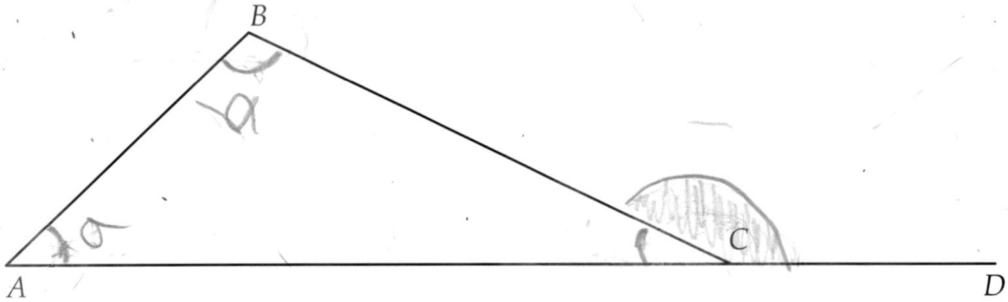

$B\hat{A}C + A\hat{B}C + A\hat{C}B = 180°$	angles of a triangle
$B\hat{C}D + A\hat{C}B = 180°$	angles on a straight line
$B\hat{C}D = B\hat{A}C + A\hat{B}C$	

To prove the angles of a quadrilateral add up to 360°:

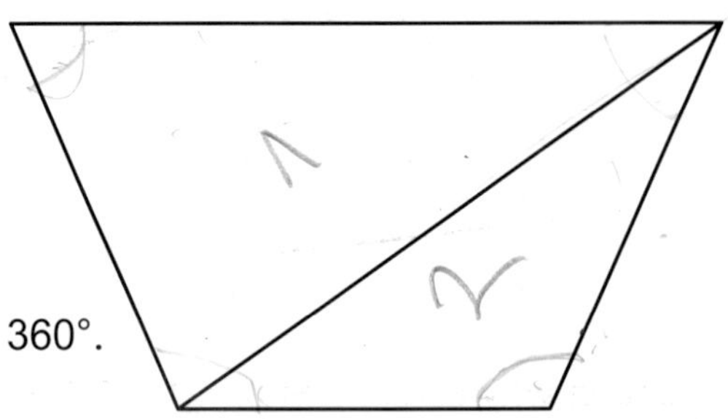

Draw in the diagonal of the quadrilateral.
This divides the quadrilateral into 2 triangles

The angles of each triangle add up to 180°.

The angles of a quadrilateral add up to 180° x 2 = 360°.

The angles in triangles & quadrilaterals ~ Questions

1. Find the size of the missing angles which are marked with letters.

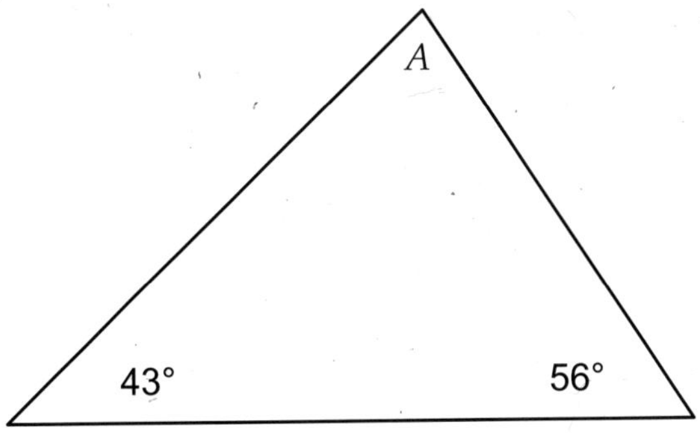

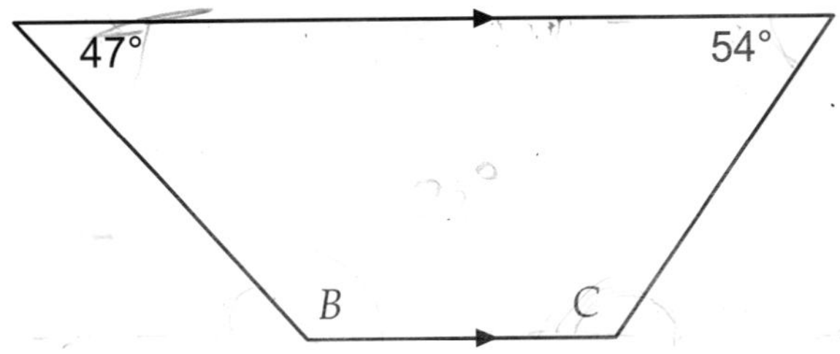

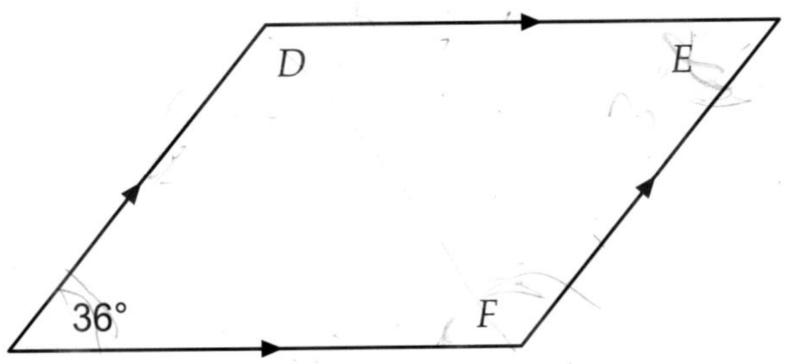

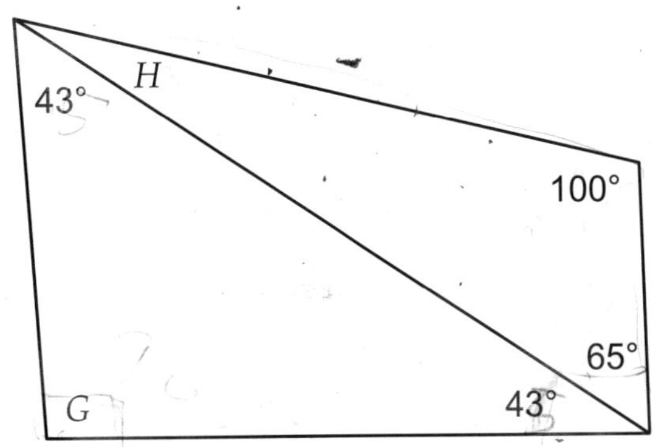

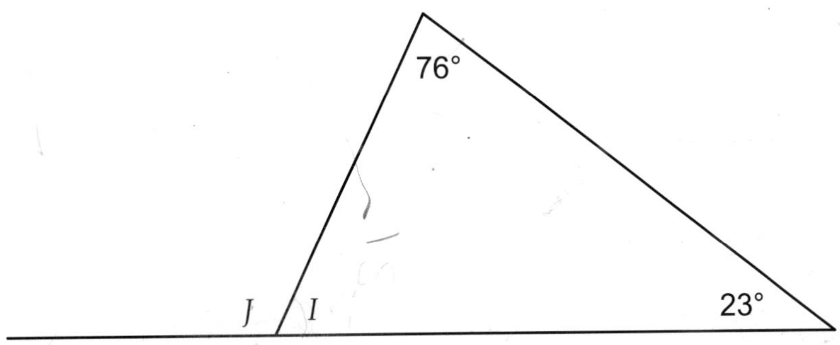

2. The diagram shows a triangle with angles as shown.

Kate says angle K should be 57°.

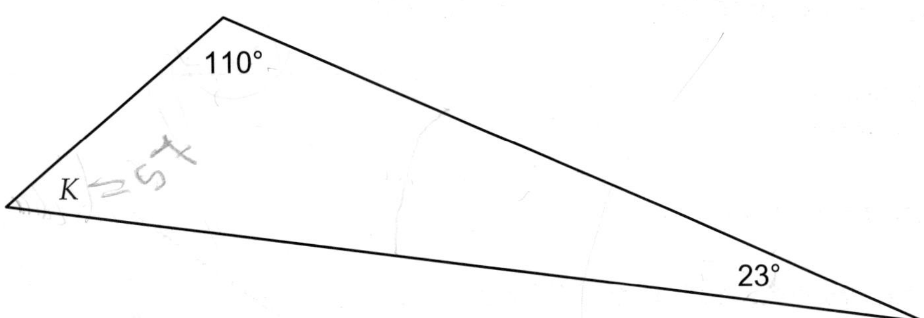

Explain why Kate must be wrong and find angle K.

Perimeter and area

A rectangle is drawn in two dimensions.

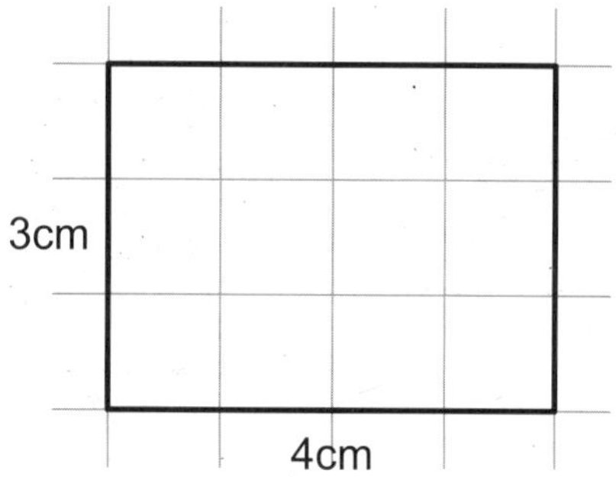

The **perimeter** of the rectangle ~ or any other shape ~ is the **total distance** around the edges of that shape.

The units for perimeter are usually millimetre (mm), centimetre (cm), metre (m) or kilometre (km).

So the perimeter of the rectangle is: **3cm + 4cm + 3cm + 4cm = 14cm**

The **area** of the rectangle ~ or any other shape ~ is a measure of the amount of space covered by the shape.

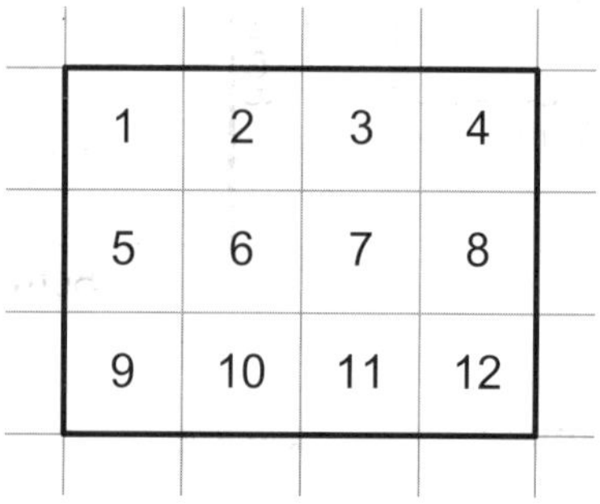

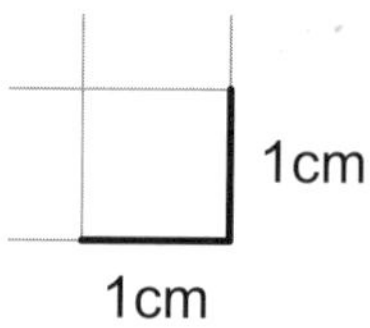

So the area of the rectangle drawn is **12cm²** and was found by counting squares.

The units for area are usually squared millimetres, squared centimetres, squared meters or squared kilometres.

You can always find the **area of a rectangle** by **multiplying the width by the length**.

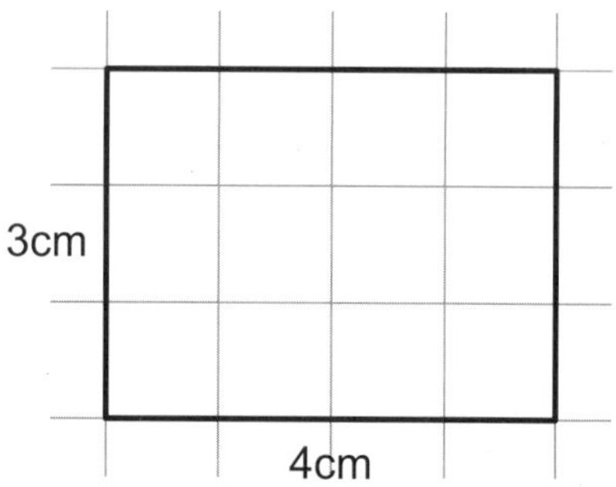

So the area of the rectangle is **3cm x 4cm = 12cm²**.

Perimeter and area ~ Questions

1. Work out the perimeters of theses shapes:

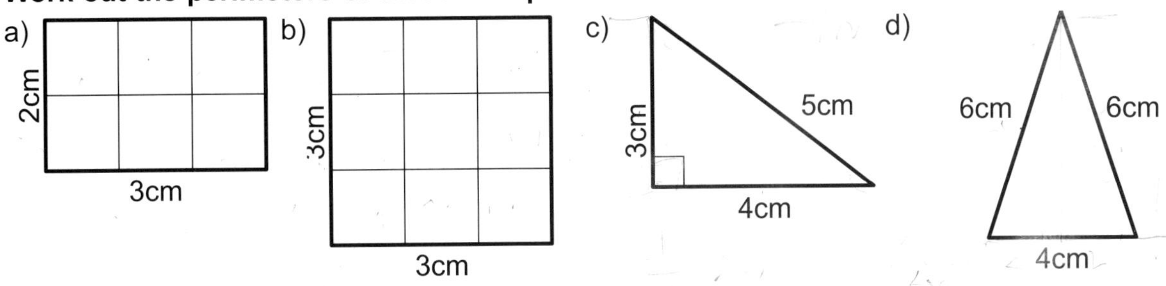

2. Find the areas of each of these shapes:

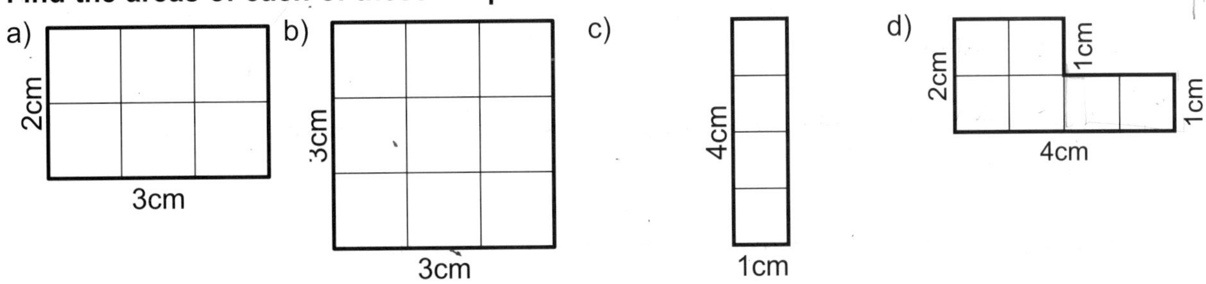

3. Work out the areas of each of these shapes:

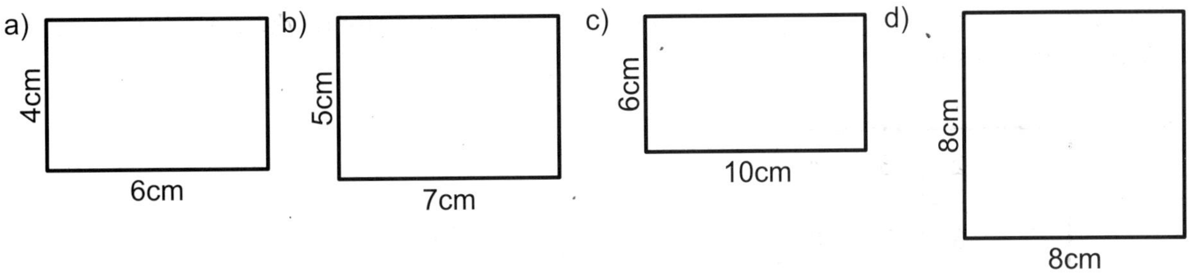

4. Estimate the area of:

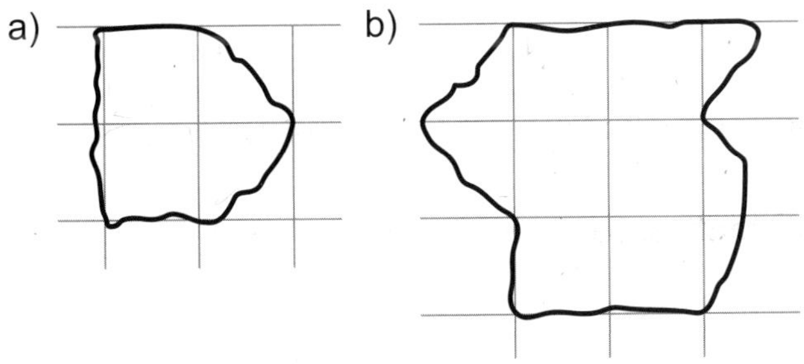

Example

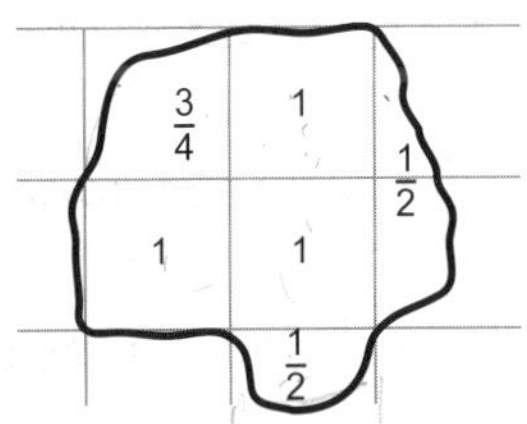

$$\text{Area} = \frac{3}{4} + 1 + 1 + 1 + \frac{1}{2} + \frac{1}{2} = 4\frac{3}{4}$$

5. a) Draw a rectangle with an area of $20cm^2$.
b) Draw another rectangle also with an area of $20cm^2$.
c) Work out the perimeter of each rectangle.

6. a) Draw a square with an area of $36cm^2$.
b) Work out the perimeter of this square.

7. Work out the area of a sports field:
which is a rectangle measuring 60 metres by 12 metres.

Area of a triangle

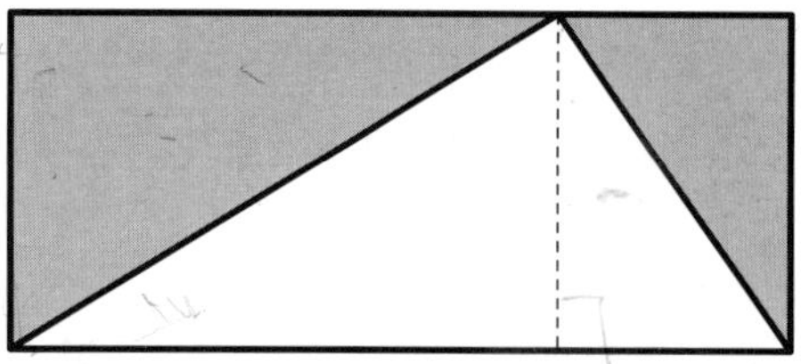

The area of a triangle is equal to $\frac{1}{2}$ of the area of the rectangle which can be drawn around it.

Area of the rectangle = base x height

Area of the triangle = $\frac{1}{2}$ base x height

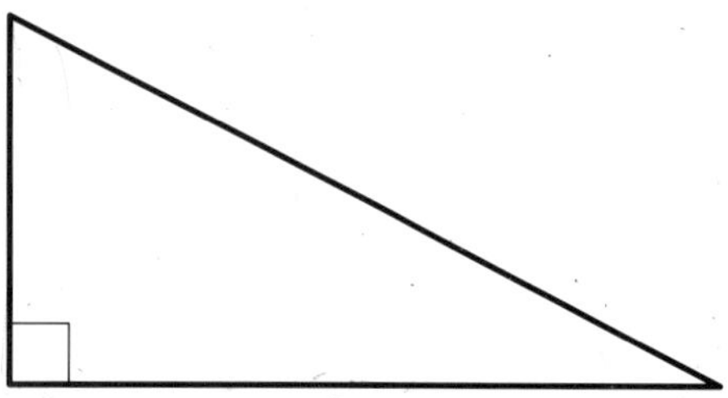

Area of triangle = $\frac{1}{2}$ base x height

$= \frac{1}{2} \times 6 \times 3$

$= 9\text{cm}^2$

Area of triangle = $\frac{1}{2}$ base x height

$= \frac{1}{2} \times 14 \times 3$

$= 21\text{cm}^2$

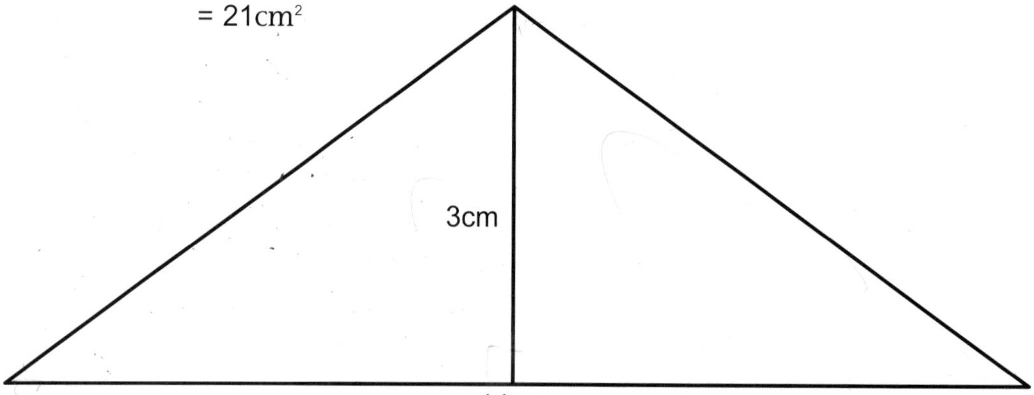

Remember AREA is square centimetres (cm^2)

Area of a triangle ~ Questions

1. Find the areas of these triangles:

a)

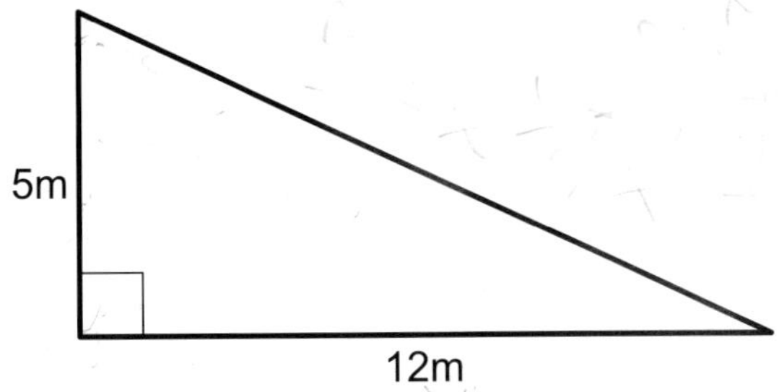

b)

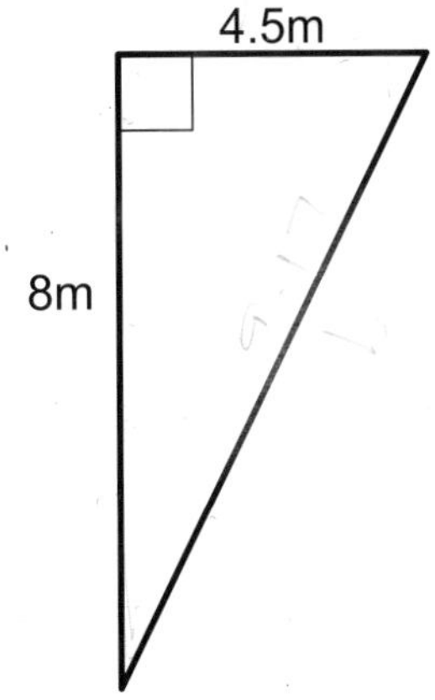

c)

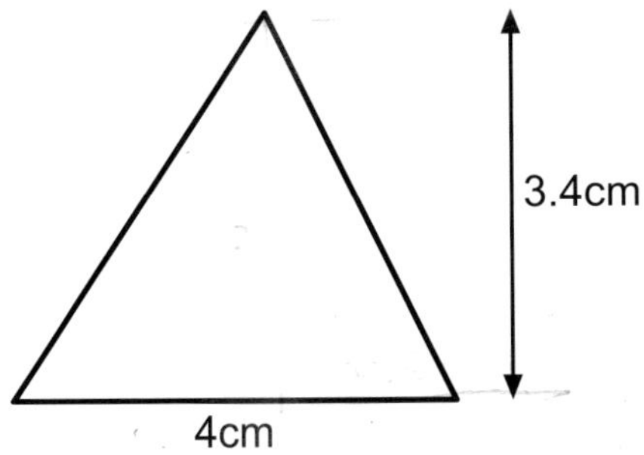

d)

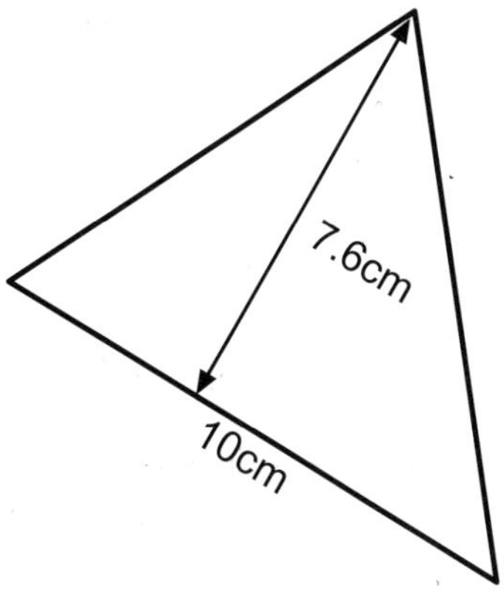

e)

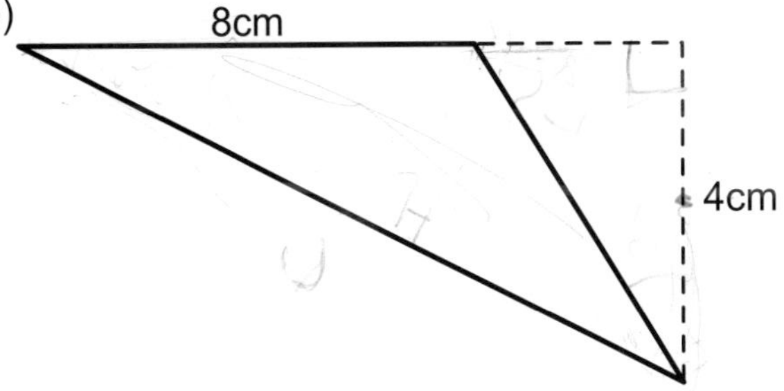

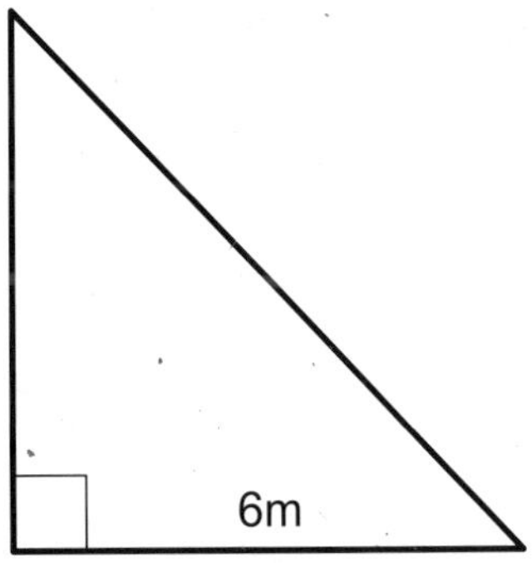

2. The area of this triangle is $12m^2$.
Find the height of the triangle.

3. Find the shaded area.

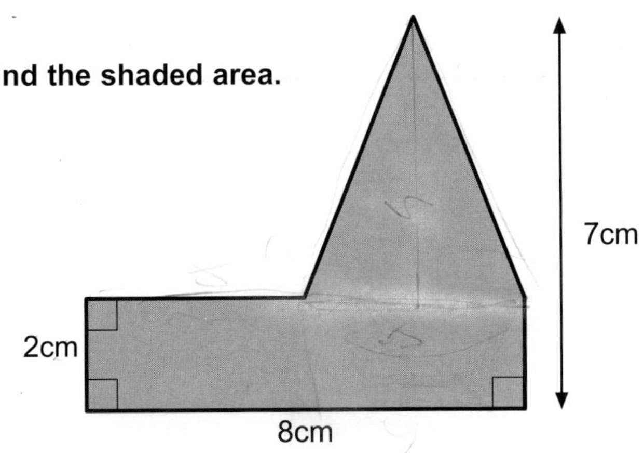

Circles

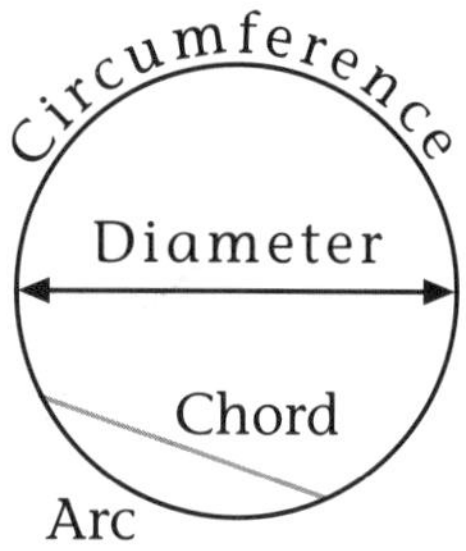

The distance from the centre to the circumference is called the radius.
The radius is half of the diameter.
A chord is a line joining two points on the circumference of a circle.
An arc is part of a circle.

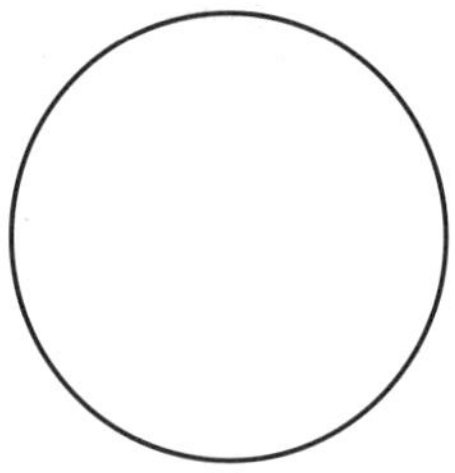

To find the circumference

The circumference is the distance all around, so we are looking for a length.
The circumference is π times the diameter.

$C = \pi D$ or $C = 2\pi r$

You need to know these formulae.

Example:

Find the circumference of a wheel with diameter 6cm.

$C = \pi D = \pi \times 6 = 18.8\text{cm}$

You may be asked to find the diameter in which case rearrange the equation

Example:

Find the diameter of a circle with circumference 128mm.

$C = \pi D$

$D = \frac{C}{\pi}$

$D = \frac{128}{\pi}$

$D = 40.7\text{mm}$

To find the area of a circle

The formula for the area of a circle is πr^2.

You need to know these formulae.

Example:

Find the area of a circle with radius 12mm.

$A = \pi r^2$
$A = \pi \times 12 \times 12$
$\doteq 452.4\text{mm}^2$

Square units for area.

Circles ~ Questions

1. Find the circumference of the following circles:

a)

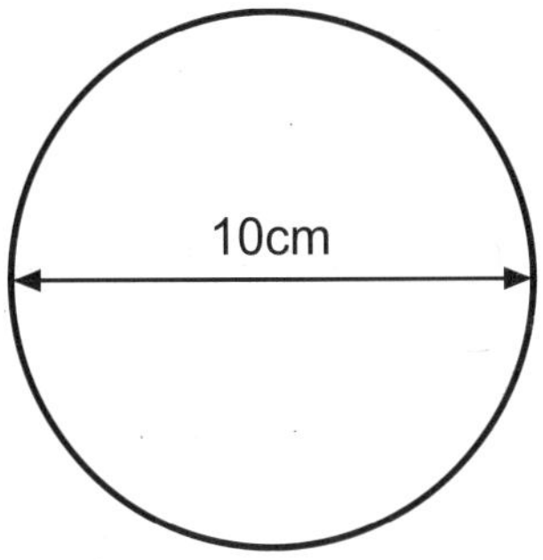

b)

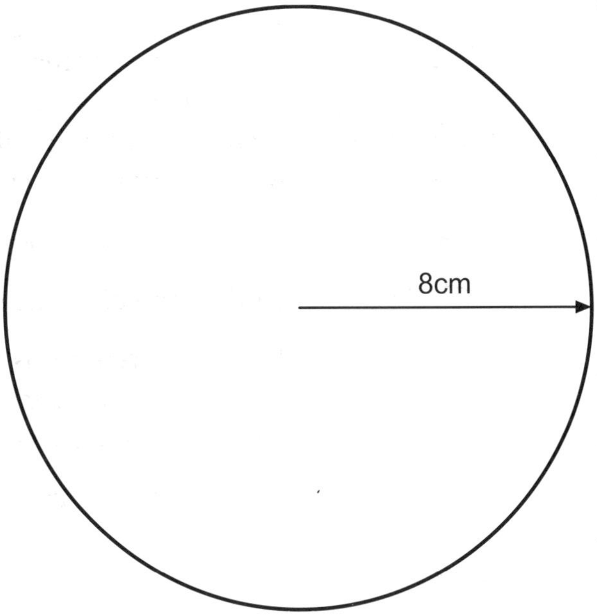

2. Find the diameter of a circle with circumference 64cm.

3. A Penny Farthing bicycle has wheels of different sizes.

The large wheel has a diameter of 1.2 metres.

a) Find the circumference of the large wheel.

b) The small wheel has a diameter of 0.3m.

Find the circumference of the small wheel.

c) How many times does the small wheel turn for each turn of the large wheel?

4. Find the area of a circle with diameter 6cm.

5. Find the diameter of a circle with area 47cm.

6. Jo wants to cut a circle from a square of material.

The circle must have area $20cm^2$.

What is the smallest possible length for the side of the square.

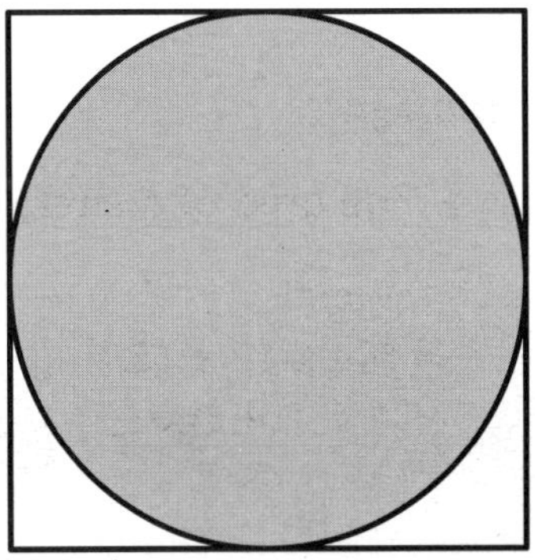

Area and volume

We can find the area of a rectangle or triangle.
Sometimes we are given more complex shapes to find the area of.

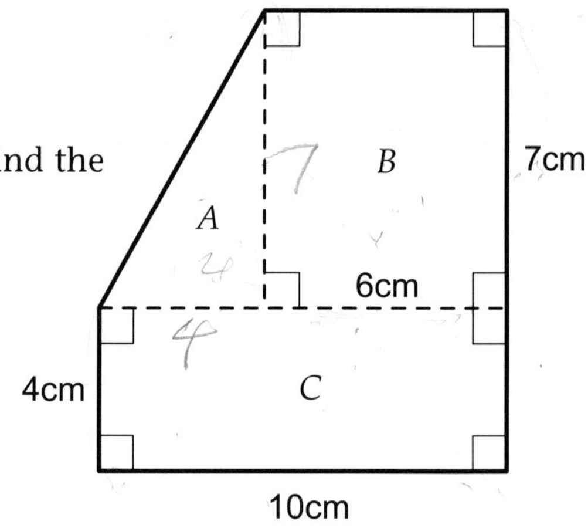

Looking at each part separately, a hard question becomes 3 easy ones with an add up at the end!

This shape is made up of 2 rectangles and a triangle.

Area of triangle $A = \frac{1}{2}$ base x height $= \frac{1}{2} \times 4 \times 7 = 14\text{cm}^2$

Area of rectangle B = length x width = $6 \times 7 = 42\text{cm}^2$

Area of rectangle C = length x width = $4 \times 10 = 40\text{cm}^2$

The total area = $A + B + C = 14 + 42 + 40\text{cm}^2 = 96\text{cm}^2$ (Notice cm^2 for an area.)

The volume of a cuboid

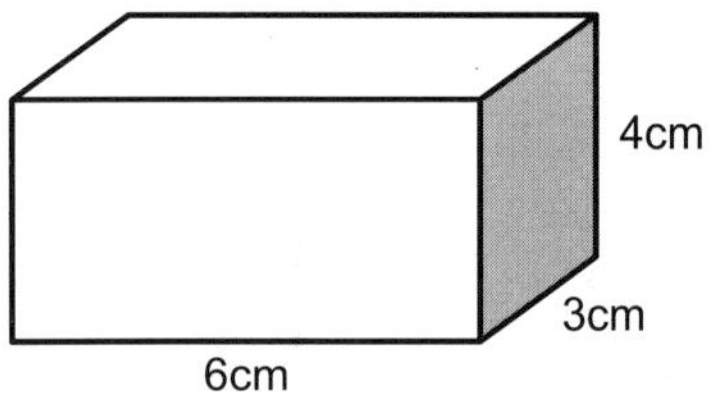

To find the volume of a cuboid, multiply the length by the width by the height.

The volume of this cuboid is $6 \times 4 \times 3\text{cm}^3 = 72\text{cm}^3$
(Notice the units for volume are cm^3 or m^3.)

The volume of a cylinder

To find the volume of this cylinder:
Volume of cylinder = area of base x height
$= \pi r^2 \times h$
$= 3.14 \times 4^2 \times 10$
$= 502.4\text{cm}^2$

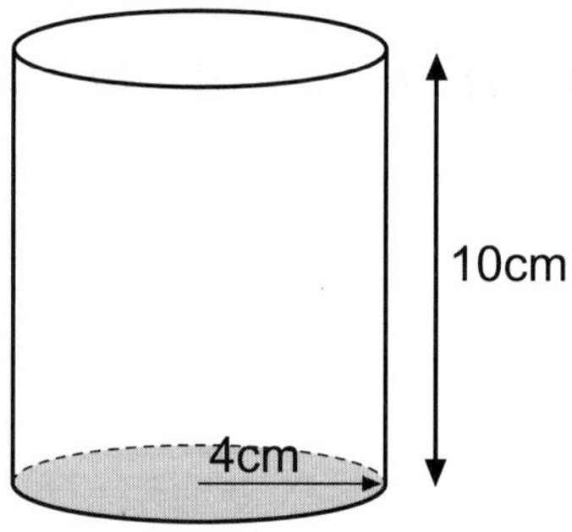

The volume of a prism

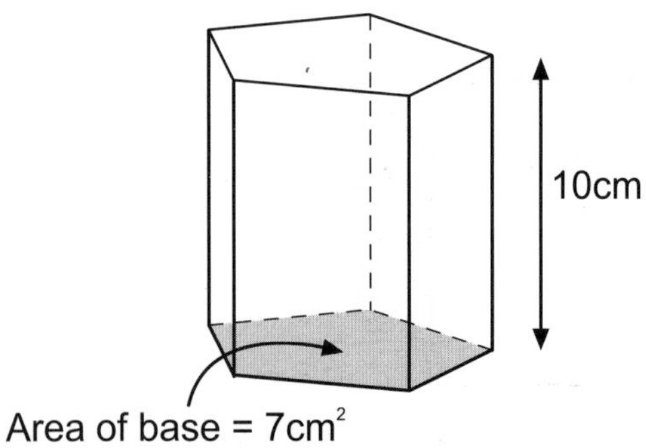

The volume of this prism is:
Volume of a prism = area of base x vertical height
$= 7 \times 10 = 70^3$

Shape and space 3

Area and volume ~ Questions

1. Find the area of the following shapes:

a)

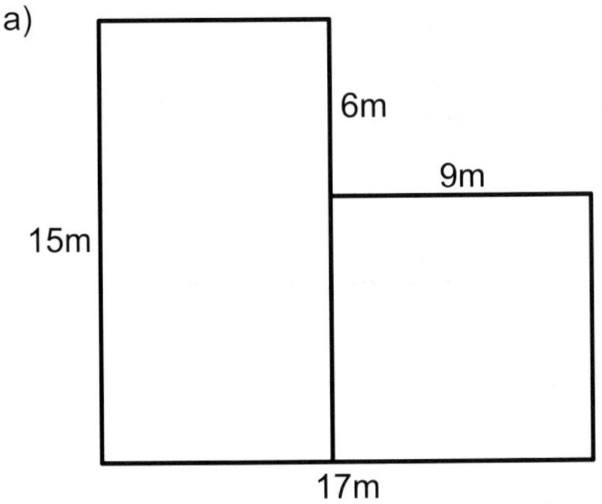

b)

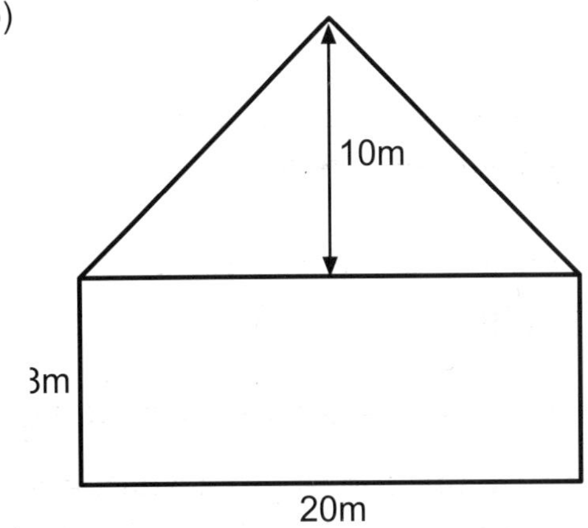

2. Find the volume of the following cuboids:

a)

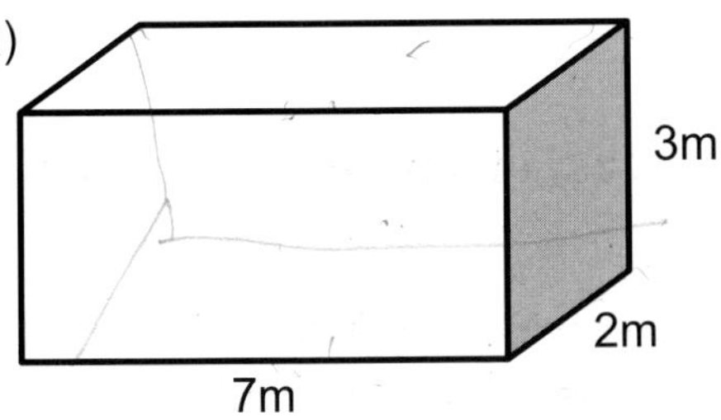

b)

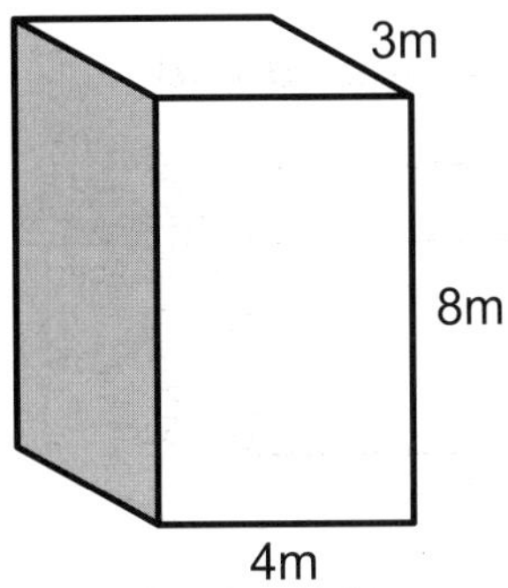

3. The diagram shows a cube with volume 15.625cm³:

Calculate the length of the side of the cube.

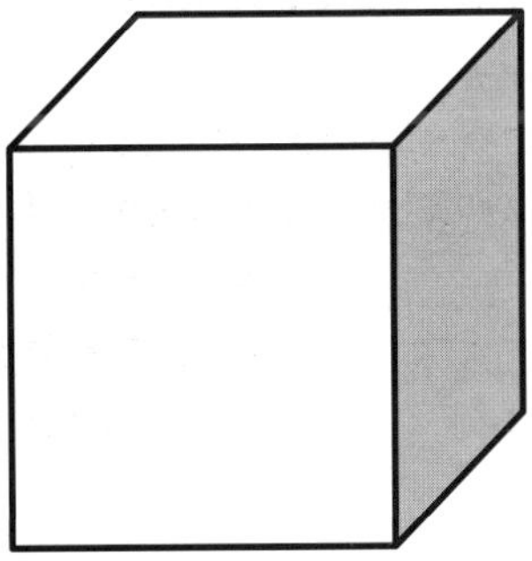

4. A cuboid of length 10cm has a square face.

If the volume of the cuboid is 160cm³,
find the width x of the cuboid.

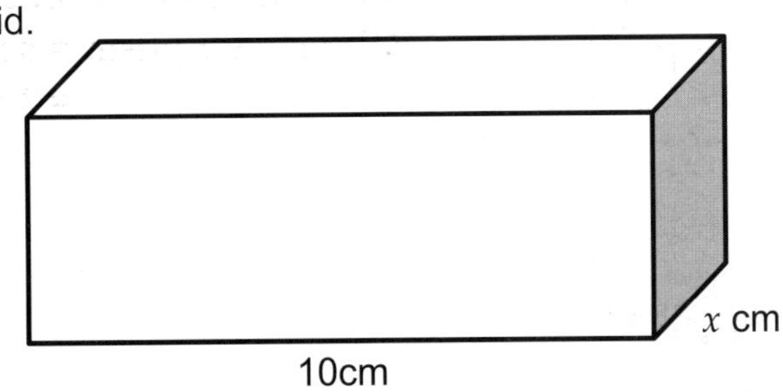

Squares on a board

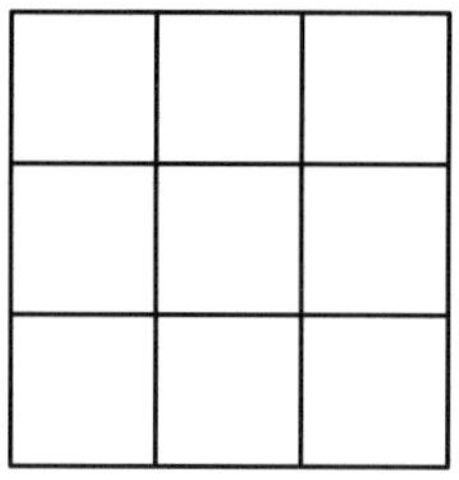

Michael says he can see **9 squares** on this board.

His sister, Vicky, says that she can see **14 squares**.

1. **Can you see all 14 of Vicky's squares?**

   Explain.

2. **How many squares are there in this square?**

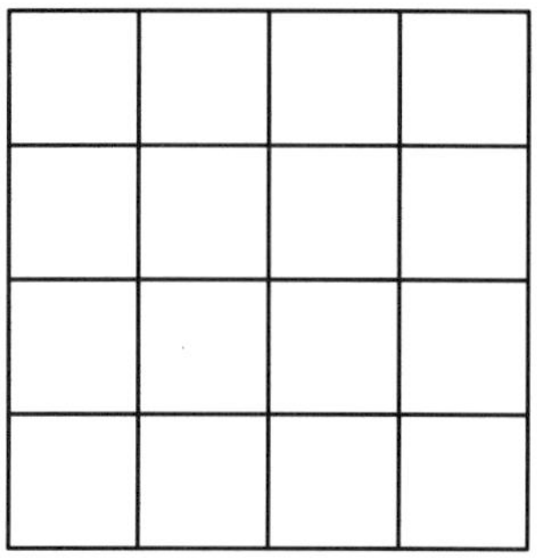

3. **How many squares are there in this square?**

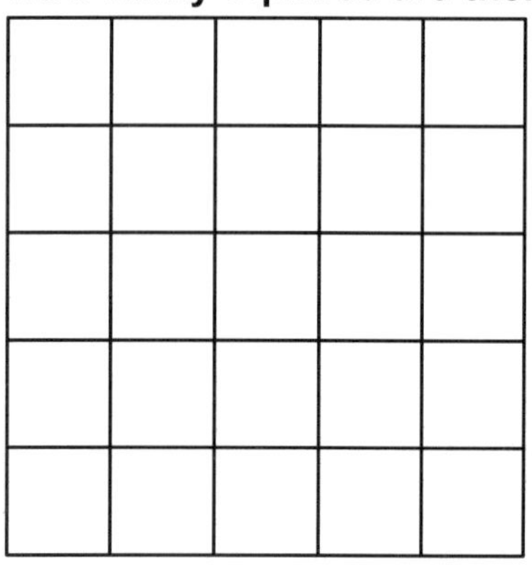

4. **Copy and complete this table:**

Size of big square	1	2	3	4	5	6	7
Number of small squares			14				

5. **How many small squares will there be in a large square of size n by n?**

Overlaps

The **overlap** of two equal squares

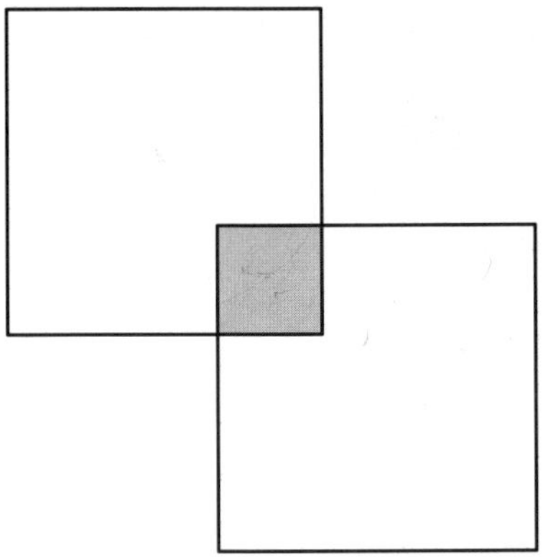

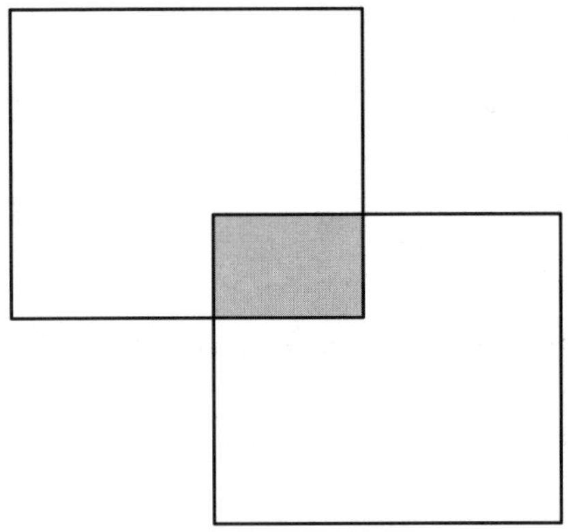

could be a **square** or it could be a **rectangle**.

The **overlap** of a square and an equilateral triangle could be

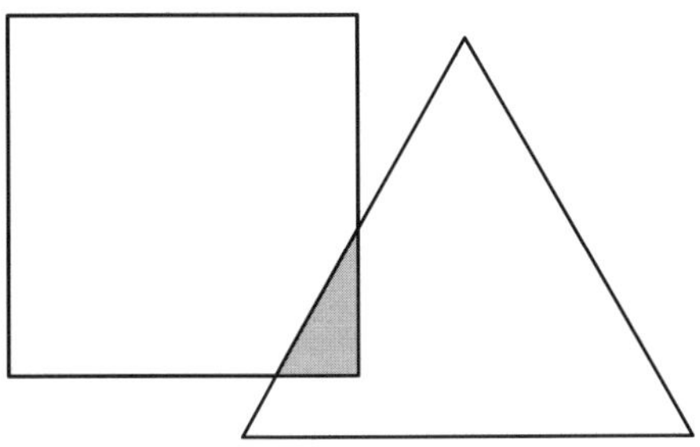

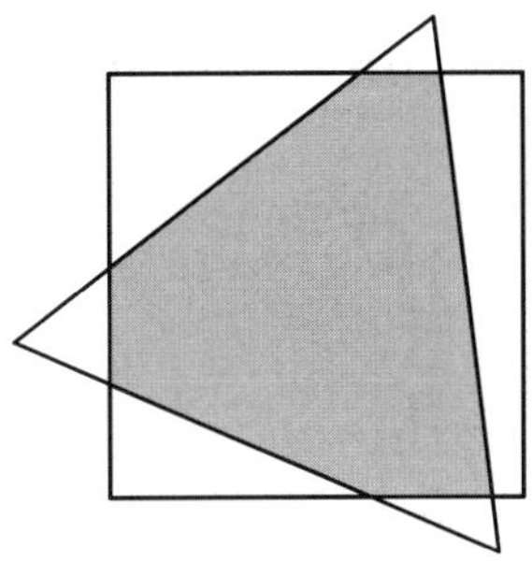

a **right angled triangle** or it could be a **hexagon**.

1. Show the shapes that can be made as the overlap of:

a) two equal sized equilateral triangles

b) two equal sized squares

c) an equilateral triangle and a square

2. Find all the shapes that can be made by the overlapping of:

a) a regular hexagon and a regular pentagon

b) a regular polygon with n sides and a regular polygon with m sides

Lists and frequency diagrams

Here is a list of the thirty girls and boys in class 9Q at Shadwell High School. The list also provides some information about them.

Girls

Name	Height (cm)	Weight (kg)
Joan	153	41
Yvonne	152	42
Jackie	162	51
Bel	162	52
Amanda	172	63
Rebecca	160	54
Alice	159	44
Jane	165	51
Lucy	166	64
Mo	171	80
Lulu	155	52
Jessie	156	53
Mary	172	82
Mel	160	74
Alison	159	63
Georgina	149	38

Boys

Name	Height (cm)	Weight (kg)
George	156	60
Terry	160	73
Joe	166	72
Tom	157	64
Billy	178	80
James	174	74
Arthur	168	81
Clem	171	106
David	158	42
Steve	182	64
Keith	179	65
Mark	155	41
Kevin	177	80
Alan	174	82

The table tells us, for instance, that:

Joan, the first girl in the list, has a height of 153cm and she weighs 41kg whilst Alan, the last boy, has a height of 174cm and weighs 82kg.

You will find questions about this list in question 1, which is across the page.

Here are the heights, in centimetres, of these 30 pupils:

153, 152, 162, 162, 172, 160, 159, 165, 166, 181, 155, 156, 172, 160, 159, 149, 163, 156, 160, 166, 157, 178, 174, 168, 171, 158, 182, 179, 155, 167.

Now we will put these heights into a table with intervals $130 \leq$ height < 140, $140 \leq$ height < 150 and so on.

Height in centimetres	Tally	Number of pupils
$140 \leq$ height < 150	/	1
$150 \leq$ height < 160	~~////~~ ~~////~~	10
$160 \leq$ height < 170	~~////~~ ~~////~~ /	11
$170 \leq$ height < 180	~~////~~ /	6
$180 \leq$ height < 190	//	2

And draw a **frequency diagram**.

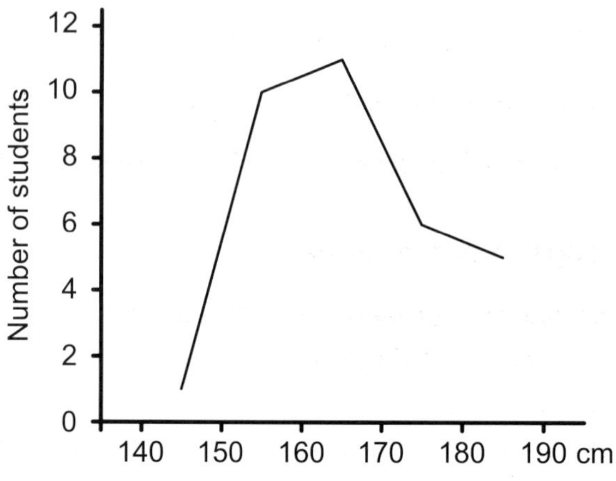

The height range with the **largest** frequency is **160 ≤** height **< 170** and is the **modal frequency**.

Lists and frequency diagrams ~ Questions

1. From the list across the page, work out:

a) the total number of girls in class 9Q at Shadwell High School

b) the total number of boys in class 9Q at Shadwell High School

c) the total number of pupils in class 9Q at Shadwell High School who have a height of:

i) 158 or more centimetres
ii) 175 or more centimetres

iii) less than 160 centimetres
iv) more than 165 centimetres

v) less than 175 centimetres but greater than 150 centimetres

d) the total number of girls in class 9Q at Shadwell High School with a weight less than 50kg

e) the total number of boys in class 9Q at Shadwell High School with a weight of more than 60kg

f) the total number of students with a weight of more than 55kg

2. a) Using the weight ranges of $30 \le$ weight < 40, $40 \le$ weight < 50 and so on, draw a frequency diagram of the weight of the pupils in Class 9Q at Shadwell High School.

b) What is the modal weight range shown by this diagram.

c) Make three other comments related to the frequency diagram.

3. a) Measure and record the heights of the pupils in your class.

b) Draw a frequency diagram to show these heights. (You may choose your own class interval if you wish or choose it to be 10 centimetres.)

c) What is the modal class interval for the heights of the pupils in your class?

d) Make at least three other comments about the results you have found.

4. Here are the miles, to the nearest 1000, driven by the set of 45 cars owned by the teachers at the High School.

33 71 32 84 36 42 12 52 62 68 20 36 41 21 55
27 21 46 77 10 32 58 12 40 63 28 81 30 22 37
17 32 73 45 86 14 60 72 44 48 25 21 29 31 22

a) Using a tally of 10 000 miles, draw a tally chart for these miles.

b) Draw a frequency diagram of the miles travelled by these cars.

c) Work out the median class range for the miles driven by these cars.

5. Work in groups of two or three.

Choose a project of your own in which you can make use of frequency diagrams.
Draw an appropriate frequency diagram.
State the modal class.
Make at least three other comments about your results.

Bar charts, bar lines & dual bar charts

Here is a **bar chart** which shows the number of people absent from class 9B last week.

The bar chart shows that there were:

5 people absent on Thursday

with similar results for other days.

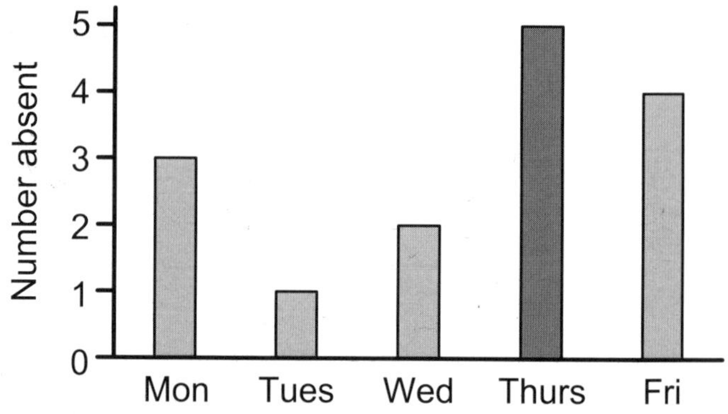

The same information about the number of people absent from class 9B last week is shown here on a **bar line** graph.

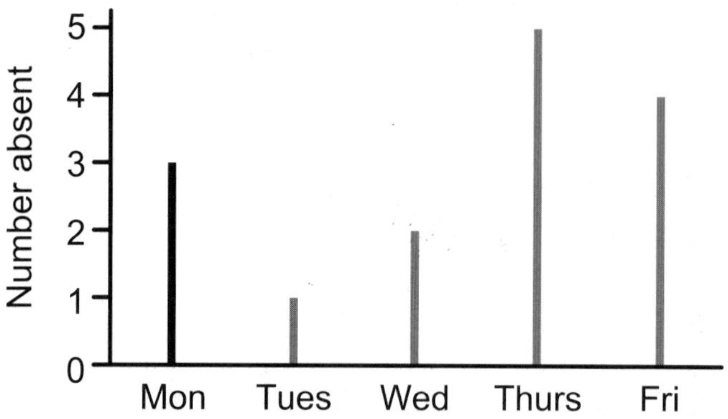

It shows us that there were:

3 people absent on Monday.

Sometimes we may wish to compare data.
This can be done by using a **dual bar chart**.

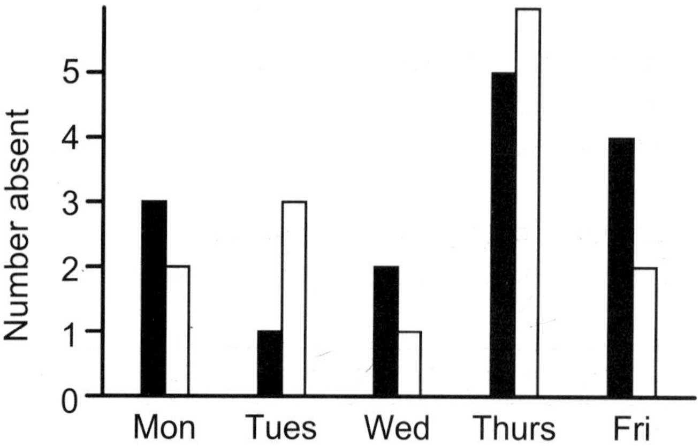

The number of people absent from class 9B last week is compared to the number absent from class 9A last week.

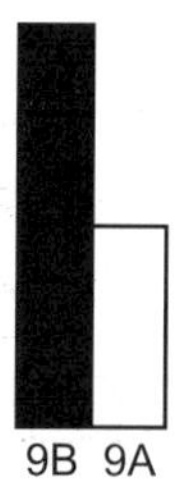

We can easily see that on Friday:

4 people were absent from class 9B whilst **2 people were absent from class 9A**.

Bar charts, bar lines & dual bar charts ~ Questions

1. Joanne asked 100 people to name their favourite colour.

She presented these results in a bar chart.

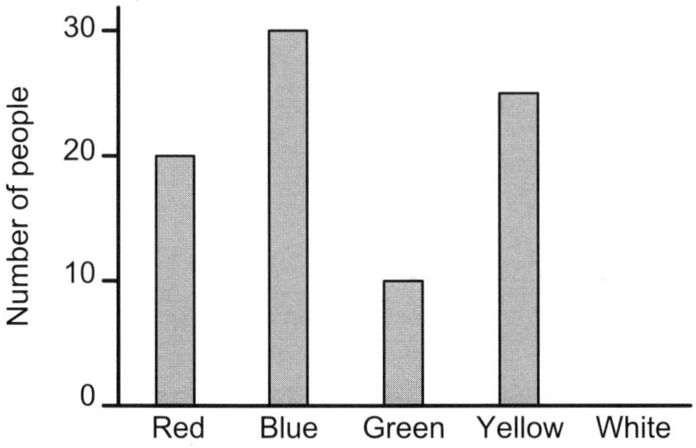

a) Copy and complete the bar chart.
b) How many people said that red was their favourite colour?
c) Out of the colours red, blue, green, yellow and white, which one did the people least like?
d) Put the six colours red, blue, green, yellow and white in the order that people like them. Start with the one people like least.

2. A school records how many pupils in Y8 and Y9 are late each day.

Each bar chart shows the results for last week.

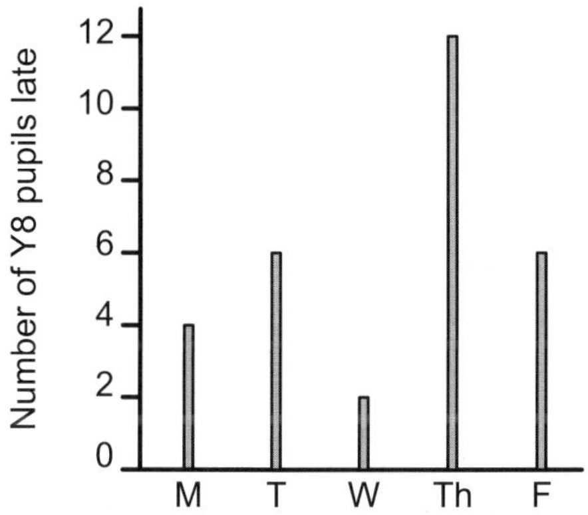

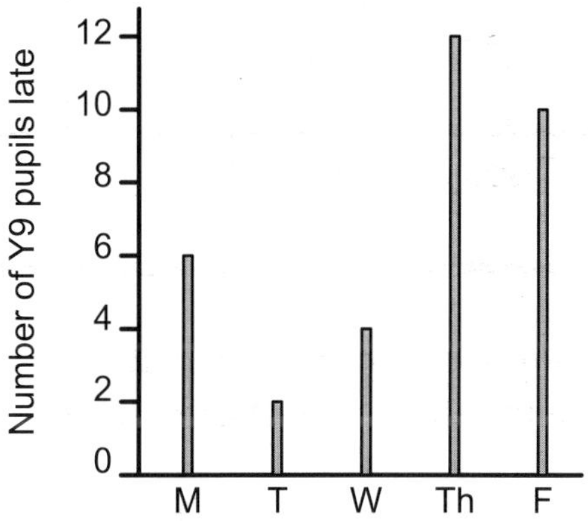

a) Which day were the number of pupils late in both year groups the same?
b) How many pupils in **Y8** were late on Wednesday?
c) **Altogether**, how many lates were recorded for **Y9** pupils?

3. Stanfield High School holds its computer club meeting each lunchtime.

Here is some information about the numbers of boys and girls attending the club on the days during one week.

Day	Monday	Tuesday	Wednesday	Thursday	Friday
Girls	7	12	15	16	9
Boys	10	11	8	20	7

a) Draw a **dual bar chart** to represent this data.
b) Work out the total number of people attending during the week.
c) On which day was there the largest difference between the number of girls and the number of boys attending the computer club?

Frequency table, averages & range

Here are the number of pupils absent from class 9A on ten different days.

4, 1, 2, 5, 1, 1, 4, 3, 2, 7

The mean of the numbers is:

$$\text{Mean} = \frac{\text{sum of the numbers}}{\text{number of numbers}}$$

So the mean is:

$$\frac{4 + 1 + 2 + 5 + 1 + 1 + 4 + 3 + 2 + 7}{10} = \frac{30}{10} = 3$$

The mode of the numbers is:

Mode is the number which occurs most often.

So the mode is perhaps best done by writing a **frequency table**.

Number	Tally	Frequency
1	///	3
2	//	2
3	/	1
4	//	2
5	//	1
6		0
7	/	1

Frequency tables can be very helpful. You can see a clearer picture.

We can see, quite clearly, that the number 1 has occurred **most often** ~ in fact it has occurred 3 times ~ so **the mode** is **1**.

The median of the numbers is:

The middle number when they are written in order.

So we get, firstly writing the numbers in order: 1 1 1 2 2 3 4 4 5 7
and then marking them off: ~~1~~ ~~1~~ ~~1~~ ~~2~~ 2 3 ~~4~~ ~~4~~ ~~5~~ ~~7~~

There are two numbers in the middle.
So we add them and divide by two.

$$\frac{2 + 3}{2} = \mathbf{2\tfrac{1}{2}}$$ which is the **median**.

The range of the set of numbers is:

Range = largest number – smallest number.

So the range is **7 – 1 = 6**.

Frequency table, averages & range ~ Questions

1. Fatima plays for the school hockey team.

In ten matches they have scored 3, 1, 0, 3, 4, 2, 3, 0, 1, 3 goals.

Work out:

a) the mode of the number of goals scored
b) the median of the number of goals scored
c) the mean of the number of goals scored
d) the range of the number of goals scored

2. A darts player throws 15 darts at the board.

The scores were: 5, 1, 20, 12, 20, 5, 18, 5, 5, 18, 8, 5, 1, 5, 18.

a) Write these scores in order, start with the lowest.
b) Find the mode for these scores.
c) Work out the median score.

3. Here are the ages, in years, of the 40 cars owned by the teachers at Shipwell Heath School.

5, 2, 3, 7, 2, 1, 4, 5, 9, 6, 2, 4, 2, 1, 8, 6, 2, 3, 2, 2
7, 2, 3, 5, 2, 1, 4, 2, 3, 2, 5, 2, 1, 7, 8, 2, 2, 3, 2, 1

a) Draw a frequency table to show these results.
b) What is the mode age of these cars?
c) Work out the median age.

4. Here are the ages of 9 children.

8, 4, 3, 11, 6, 7, 9, 8, 10

a) Work out the mean age of these children.
b) Work out the range of the ages of these children.
c) State the value of the mode age of these children.

5. Here is Miss Straw's record of the marks scored by the pupils from her class in a short spelling test.

Mark	4	5	6	7	8	9	10
Number of pupils	2	3	8	4	6	4	2

a) Write down the mode of these marks.
b) Work out the median mark.
c) Work out the range of these marks.
d) Work out the mean of these marks.

Line graphs

The table shows the temperature, in degrees Centigrade, in Birmingham at midday during the first week in June.

June	1	2	3	4	5	6	7
Temperature (°C)	13	17	15	12	13	16	18

We can show data such as the set above on a **line graph**. Here are two ways of doing so:

First way:

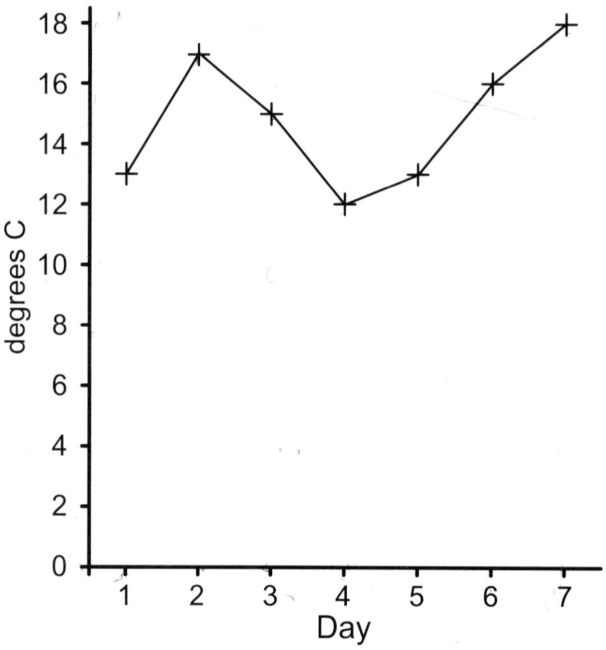

On this graph the temperature scale always starts at 0 degrees centigrade.

Second way:

This graph gives us more space on the vertical axis.

The break point in the vertical axis shows that the scale goes straight from 0 degrees to 10 degrees.

This means a break from 0 to 10.

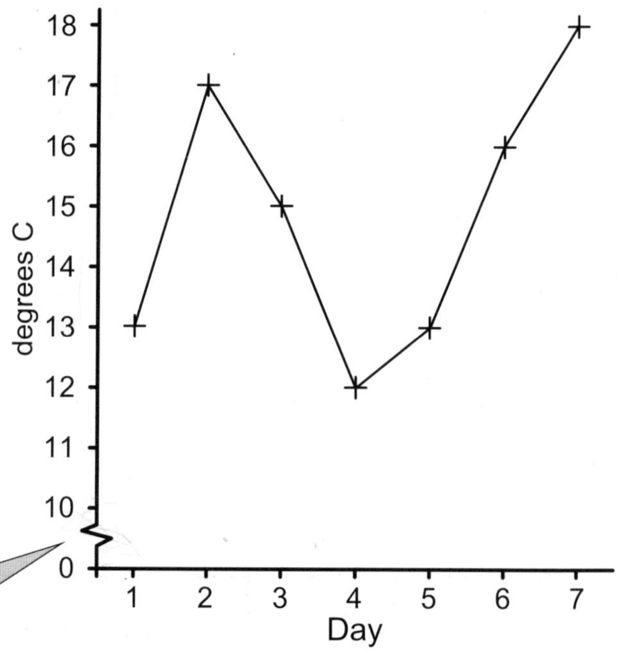

You may be asked questions in which you are invited to comment on these two types of representing data, or you may be asked to draw graphs with and/or without a broken axis. There are also questions where you are given a **line graph** and asked to make some form of comment about it.

Line graphs ~ Questions

1. Draw line graphs to represent each of the following:

a) The number of letters delivered to a guest house one week:

Mon	Tues	Wed	Thur	Fri	Sat	Sun
12	25	15	19	23	20	0

b) The noon temperature, in °C, in Cambridge:

Temperature (°C)	22	18	17	21	21	24	23
July	1	2	3	4	5	6	7

2. a) Draw a line graph to show the monthly temperature in °C for Tenerife, shown in the table below:

Temperature (°C)	19	20	21	23	25	27	28	28	27	25	22	20
Month	J	F	M	A	M	J	J	A	S	O	N	D

b) Work out the mean monthly temperature for Tenerife.

3. This graph shows the temperature, in °C, at noon during the first seven days of June in Swansea.

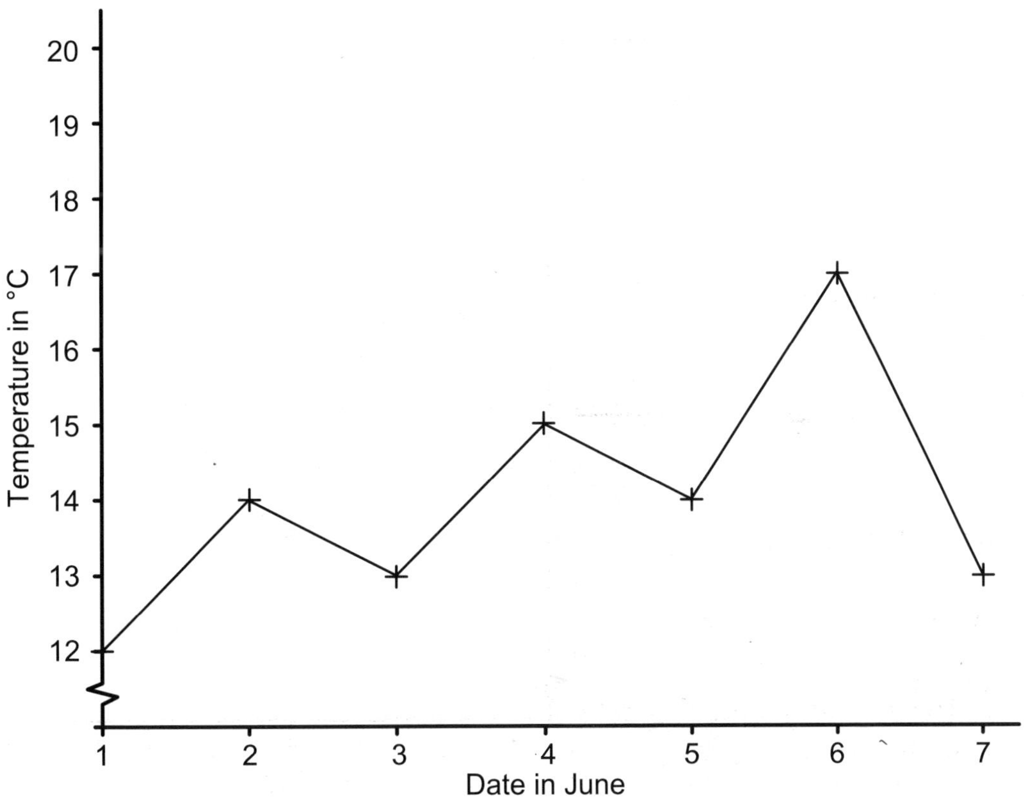

a) On which of these days was the noon temperature at its lowest?
b) What was the range in the temperature?
c) Work out the mean noon temperature.

Averages

Averages are used to represent a group. There are 3 types of average:

The Mode ~ the most common or popular data value.
(Sometimes called the modal value)
This is valuable because it can be the average for something which is not a number.
E.g. the modal hair colour is brown.

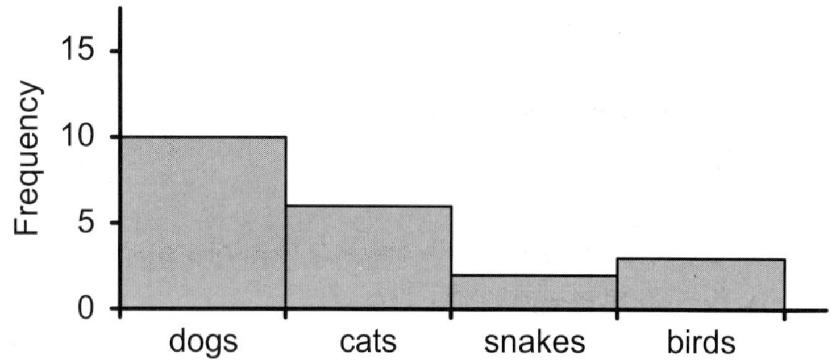

For this class the modal pet is the dog.

The Median

For this average the numbers must be in order. Choose the middle one.
E.g. 9 pupils from year 7 are given the following amounts of money:

£1	£3	£5	£2	£4	£1	£9	£6	£3
Place the amounts in order.								
£1	£1	£2	£3	£3	£4	£5	£6	£9

The median is the middle one: £3. This average is not affected by extremes.

The Mean

To find the mean: 1. Find the total for all of the sets of data.
2. Divide by the number of pieces of data you have.

The mean amount of pocket money for the year 7 pupils is:

$$\frac{£1 + £3 + £5 + £2 + £4 + £1 + £9 + £6 + £3}{9} = \frac{34}{9}$$

= 3.777 or £3.78

Money ~ so the sensible answer is correct to the nearest 1p.

The Range

This tells us how far the data is spread.
For our year 7 pupils the range of pocket money is:
The biggest take away the smallest £9 – £1 = £8

Averages ~ Questions

1. **The number of goals scored by football team A over 9 weeks is given below:**

   1 1 3 2 0 0 0 0 7

   Find:
   a) The mode.
   b) The mean number of goals scored.
   c) The median number of goals scored.
   d) The range of the goals scored.
   e) The manager of team A writes an article for the local press. Which average would he use to make the team appear good? Give a reason for your answer.
   f) The team manager for team B who are to play team A next week tells his team the average number of goals scored by team A. Which average should he use? Give a reason for your answer.

2. **Angie's friends have heights as given below:**

   125cm 136cm 124cm 127cm 126cm 137cm 124cm 125cm 130cm

   Tom says:

   Explain why Tom must be wrong.

   Use your calculator to work out:
   a) The mean height for Angie's friends.
   b) The modal height for Angie's friends.
   c) The median height for Angie's friends.
   d) The range for the heights of Angie's friends.

3. **Ten students were given 2 different Maths tests.**
   Their results are shown below:

Test A	32	47	25	54	90	34	42	67	36	29
Test B	37	43	57	49	45	39	54	59	42	48

   Which test did the students find more difficult? Give a reason for your answer.

4. **Three friends choose differently priced meals from the menu.**
   The average price of the 3 meals was £10.
   What might each individual meal have been priced at?

5. **Ben's marks for 4 maths tests were 62, 74, 69, 63.**

   a) What was Ben's average mark?
   b) What mark does he need to get on his next test to raise his average to 70?

Pie charts

A pie chart represents all of the data.

A circle is divided into parts called sectors.

To draw a pie chart

The following table shows the different types of transport 36 children use to travel to school.

Car	Bus	Walk	Bike	Other
10	8	12	4	2

Each part of the circle is $\frac{360°}{36} = 10°$.

So each child will be represented by 10°.

Transport Type	Pupils		Angle
Car	10	10 x 10	100°
Bus	8	8 x 10	80°
Walk	12	12 x 10	120°
Bike	4	4 x 10	40°
Other	2	2 x 10	20°

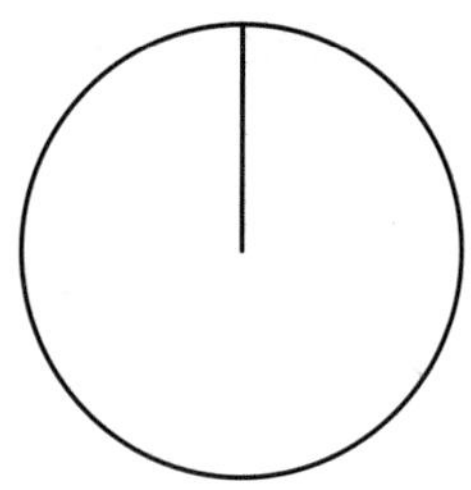

1. Draw a large circle.
2. Draw in a radius.
   (Join the centre to the circumference).

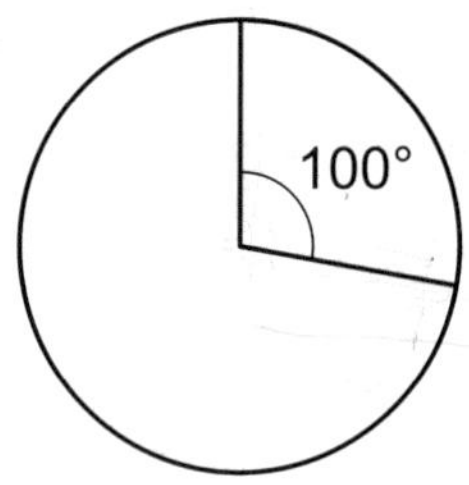

3. Using your protractor or angle measurer with this line as your base line draw an angle of 100° for the cars.
4. Move your protractor/angle measurer to the next line and measure the angle for bus 80°.
5. Continue until you have drawn in all of the angles.
6. If you have worked accurately, the last angle of 20° should take you back to the original radius.
7. Measure it to check.
8. Give your pie chart a **title**.
9. Label the sections or give it a key.

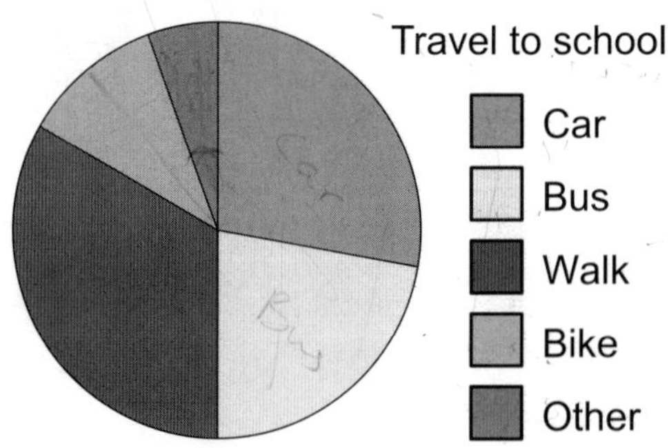

Pie charts ~ Questions

1. Elmhurst School are considering changing their uniform.

Pupils voted for the colour they preferred.

The results for form 9A are shown below.

Red	Black	Blue	Green	Maroon
5	12	9	3	7

a) How many pupils voted?

b) What angle should represent 1 pupil in the pie chart?

c) Draw the pie chart for their results.

2. A youth club spends £300 on a disco.

The DJ costs £100.

The printing and adverts cost £60.

The room hire cost £90.

Refreshments cost £50.

Draw a pie chart to show what the youth club spent on the disco.

3. A boy spends his day on the following activities.

Sleeping 9 hours

Eating 2 hours

School 6 hours

Homework 2 hours

Recreation 5 hours

Draw a pie chart to show these activities.

Did you remember the title and key?

Using a pie chart

You may be given a pie chart and asked to find information from it.

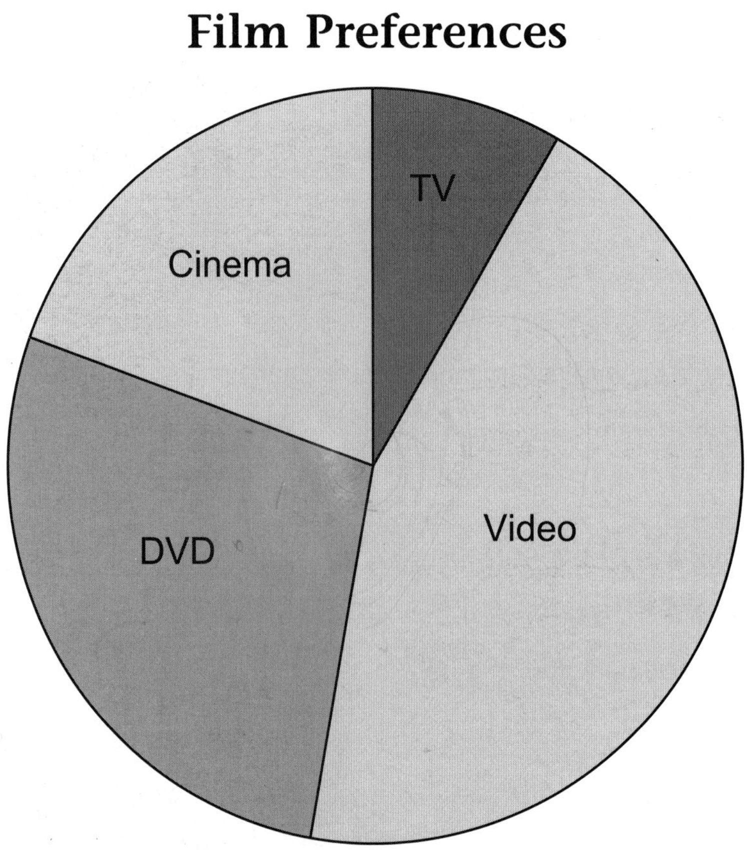

This pie chart shows the results of a survey in which 180 people were asked how they would prefer to view a film.

We can see that the most popular was video as it has the biggest sector and the least popular was TV as it has the smallest.

As 180 people took part in the survey we can work out how many are represented by each sector.

To find out how many people prefer watching a DVD:

1. Use your angle measurer or protractor to measure the angle for DVD. It should be 100°.

2. In the full pie chart, 360° represents 180 people.

   So $\frac{360°}{180°} = 2°$ represents 1 person.

3. If 2° represents 1 person, 100° represents $\frac{100}{2} = 50$ people.

Using a pie chart ~ Questions

1. The pie chart shows the number of pupils choosing different sports.

120 pupils took part in the survey.

a) Which sport was most popular?

b) How many degrees represent 1 pupil on the pie chart?

c) How many pupils chose football?

d) How many pupils chose hockey?

e) How many pupils chose athletics?

f) How many pupils chose swimming?

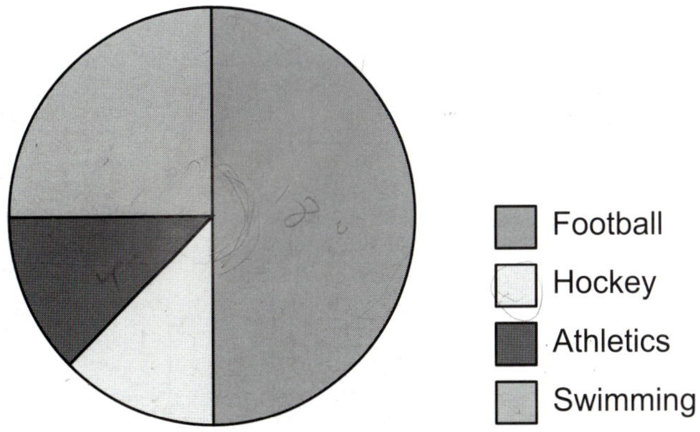

2. A class of 30 students were asked where they were going on holiday and the results are shown in the pie chart.

a) Which is the most popular destination?

b) What angle represents 1 person on the pie chart?

c) How many people will travel to the USA?

d) How many will not leave Great Britain?

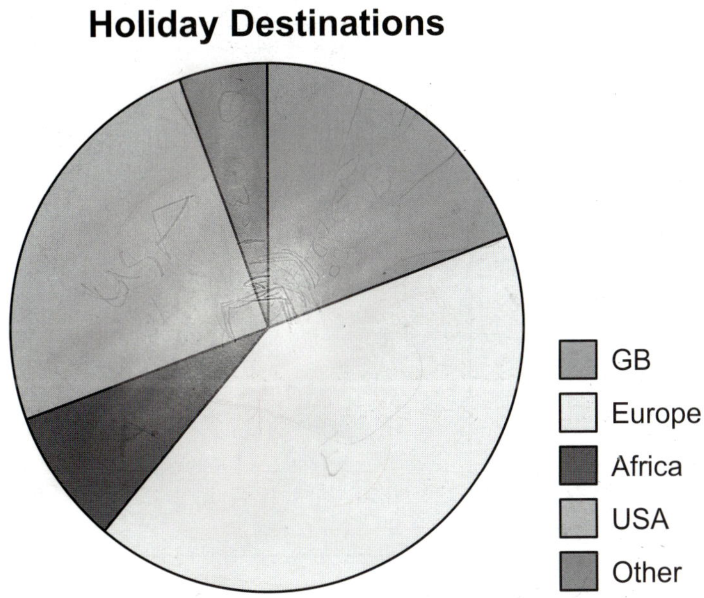

3. There are 180 pupils in Y9 at Tane School.

Their results in KS3 Maths tests were:

Level	3	4	5	6	7	8
Number	4	20	73	60	14	9

Draw a pie chart which shows this information.

Correlation and scatter diagrams

A scatter diagram is used to show two sets of data so that we can compare them.
The correlation between the two sets of data means there is a connection.
There are three types:

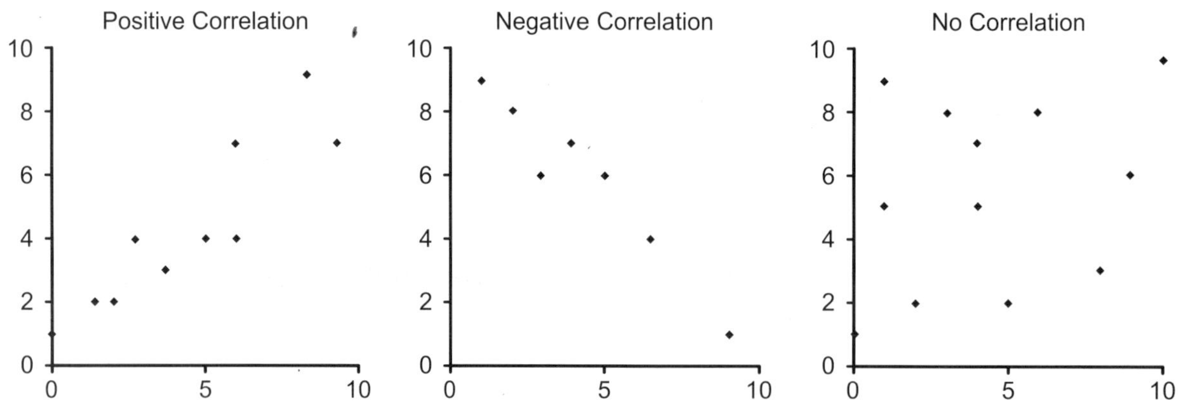

Example:
The following marks were achieved by pupils on their French and German papers.

French	5	6	3	8	9	2	4	7	6	7
German	4	6	5	7	8	3	6	6	4	5

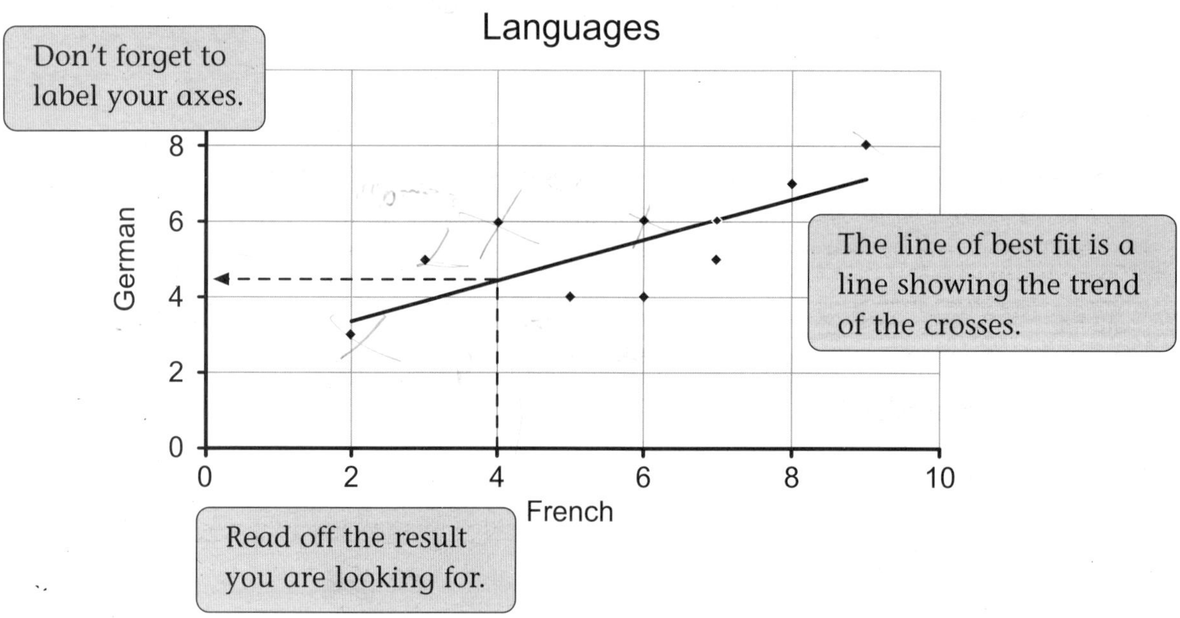

There is a high positive correlation.
Mark achieved 4 on the French test.

We can estimate his mark on the German test by reading off from the line of best fit.
Reading from the line of best fit, Mark should have achieved 4.5 for German.

Correlation and scatter diagrams ~ Questions

1. Samantha scored 5 marks on the French test.

What mark would you expect her to obtain in German? (Look at the previous page.)

2. George scored 6 marks in German.

What would you expect him to achieve in French? (Look at the previous page.)

3. A shop keeper is looking at the price of small sweets and the numbers sold.

He collects some data.

a) Draw a scatter graph for the prices and numbers sold.

b) Draw a line of best fit.

c) Describe the correlation.

d) If an item is priced at 5p, how many can he expect to sell?

Price	2	3	6	7	1	7	2	3	4	9
Number sold	7	8	5	2	9	3	6	4	3	2

4. Jean sells ice cream.

She thinks there may be a relationship between the amount she sells and the temperature. Use the information in the table below to draw a scatter diagram.

Temperature in °C	1	5	10	20	17	12	4	19	24	15	6
Number of ice creams sold	10	15	20	50	45	26	12	49	60	30	12

a) Draw a line of best fit.

b) Describe the correlation.

c) If the temperature is 18°C, how many ice creams can she expect to sell?

d) On Thursday she sold 14 ice creams.
Estimate what the temperature might have been?

Frequency diagrams

Discrete data is items of data which we can count:
e.g. number of children, number of chairs or books.

Quantities like length, weight or time are **continuous**.
This means we can never give an exact value.
We are limited by the accuracy with which we can measure.

When we record continuous data we have to round off.

Example: the heights of 20 plants have been recorded, correct to the nearest millimetre.

20.1	24.6	34.2	28	21.7	22.3	38.2	22.9	36.0	35.4
29.7	28.9	15.6	16.2	21.4	18.2	25.7	27.3	33.4	26.2

Construct a grouped frequency table.

Height x cm	Tally	Frequency
$15.0 \leq x < 20.0$		
$20.0 \leq x < 25.0$	/	
$25.0 \leq x < 30.0$		
$30.0 \leq x < 35.0$		
$35.0 \leq x < 40.0$		

This / represents 20.1.

This group contains 30.0 but not 35.0.

Height x cm	Tally	Frequency
$15.0 \leq x < 20.0$	///	3
$20.0 \leq x < 25.0$	~~////~~ /	6
$25.0 \leq x < 30.0$	~~////~~ /	6
$30.0 \leq x < 35.0$	//	2
$35.0 \leq x < 40.0$	///	3

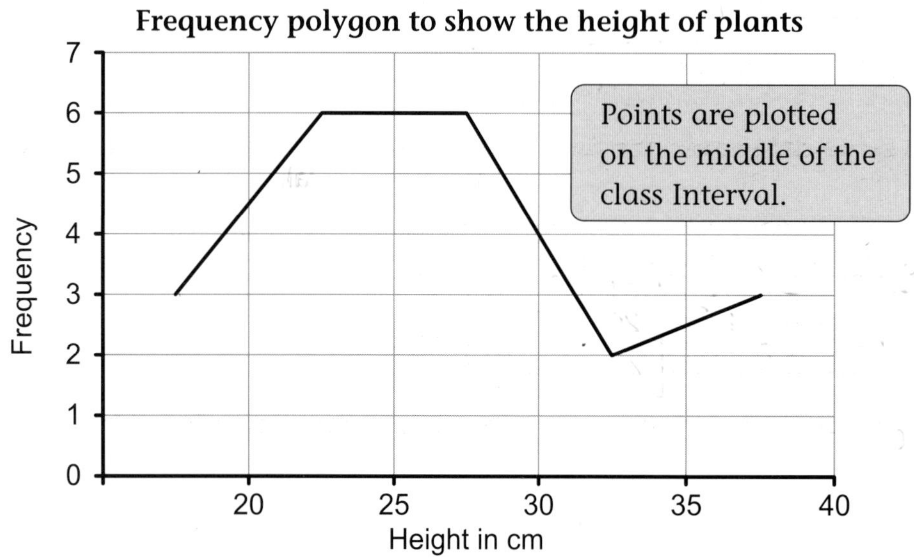

Frequency diagrams ~ Questions

1. **Tom collected the average amount of time in minutes spent by pet owners walking the dog.**

5	7	12	35	45
60	30	10	55	25
30	32	23	28	11
50	58	15	23	36
10	18	42	44	31

Copy and complete the frequency table.

Time in Minutes	Tally	Frequency
$0 < x \leq 10$		
$10 < x \leq 20$		
$20 < x \leq 30$		
$30 < x \leq 40$		
$40 < x \leq 50$		
$50 < x \leq 60$		

Draw a frequency polygon to represent the data.

2. **Jenny collected some data about temperature measured in °C during a science experiment.**

10	14	5	10	15
30	24	17	12	3
6	18	25	32	19
21	17	29	9	11
7	13	18	21	12

Draw a frequency polygon to represent the data.

3. **Yoland collected some data about the time, in minutes, it takes the people in her form to travel to school.**

25	5	30	22	17	40	31	30	16	18
13	12	4	8	10	32	20	17	19	21
32	18	24	19	16	15	43	13	17	12

Using intervals $0 \leq x < 5$, $5 \leq x < 10$, etc, draw a frequency polygon to represent the data.

Probability 1

Probability tells us how likely something is to happen.
All probabilities lie between 0 and 1.

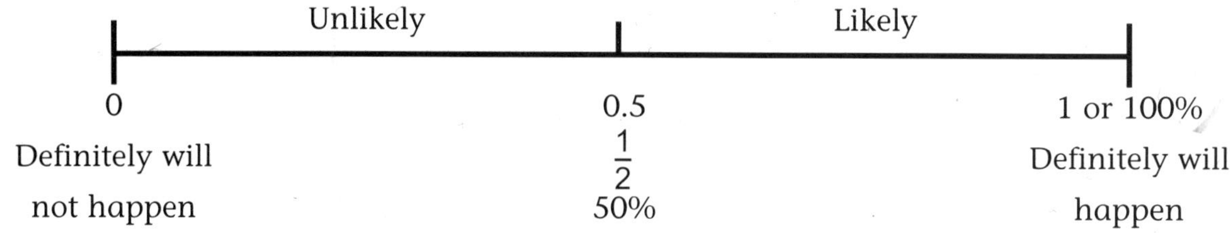

The probability of an event: P(event)

$$= \frac{\text{number of ways of an outcome happening}}{\text{Number of possible outcomes}}$$

What is the probability of throwing a 3 on an ordinary dice?

The possible outcomes are 1, 2, 3, 4, 5, and 6.

There is 1 possible way of getting a 3.

So the probability of throwing a 3 is $\frac{1}{6}$.

What is the probability of throwing an even number?

The possible outcomes are 1, 2, 3, 4, 5, and 6.

The possible even numbers are 2, 4, 6.

So the probability of throwing an even number is $\frac{3}{6} = \frac{1}{2}$.

We write P(event) $= \frac{1}{2}$.

What is the probability of throwing a 7 when you roll an ordinary dice?

This is impossible, so P(7) = 0.

Outcomes

It is useful to be able to list all of the possible outcomes.

Use a table!

Possible outcomes on tossing a coin and throwing a dice					
Head, 1	Head, 2	Head, 3	Head, 4	Head, 5	Head, 6
Tail, 1	Tail, 2	Tail, 3	Tail, 4	Tail, 5	Tail, 6

If you have a system you are less likely to miss any.

Probability 1 ~ Questions

1. A bag contains 3 red beads, 2 blue beads and 1 black bead.

Jo picks a bead. What is the probability that it is:

a) a black bead?
b) a red bead?
c) a white bead?

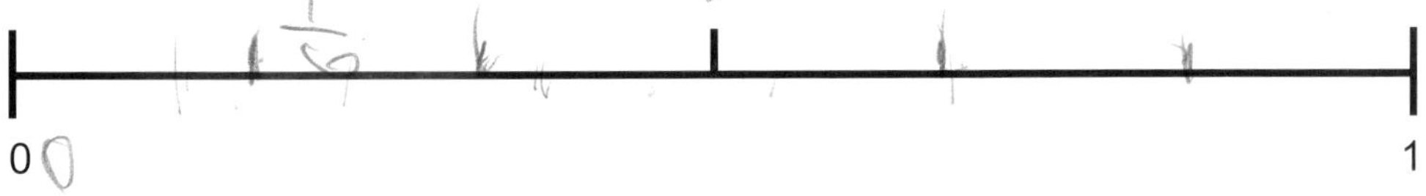

d) Copy the probability line and mark the probability of choosing:

i) a red bead ii) a blue bead iii) a white bead

2. John's café sells sandwiches and drinks.

Sandwich Menu	**Drinks Menu**
Sausage	Tea
Egg	Coffee
Bacon	Milk
Tomato	

A customer is equally likely to choose any of the items.

a) List all of the possible outcomes if I choose a sandwich and a drink.
b) How many possible outcomes are there?
c) What is the probability of someone choosing a sausage sandwich?
d) What is the probability of choosing milk?
e) What is the probability of choosing an egg sandwich and a cup of coffee?

3. The hexagonal spinner shown below is spun.

a) Which number is most likely to be spun?
b) Which number is least likely to be spun?
c) What is the probability of a 2?
d) What is the probability of a 3?
e) What is the probability of a 1?
f) What is the probability of a 7?

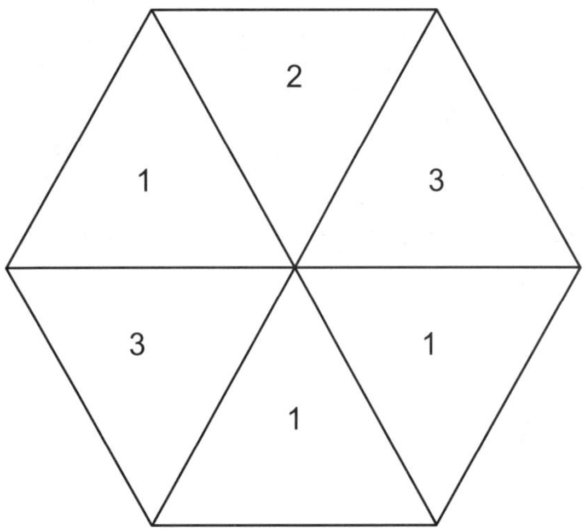

Probability 2

The sum of the probabilities for all the possible events is 1.

Example: A Mathematics prize is awarded to a pupil in the school.
If the probability that a girl wins the prize is 0.7 then the probability that a boy wins the prize is 1 – 0.7 = 0.3.

Sometimes we are looking at combinations of events.
The probability that a girl wins the prize for mathematics is 0.7.
The probability that a boy wins the prize for English is 0.8.
We use a tree diagram to help us to work out the probability for each possible outcome.

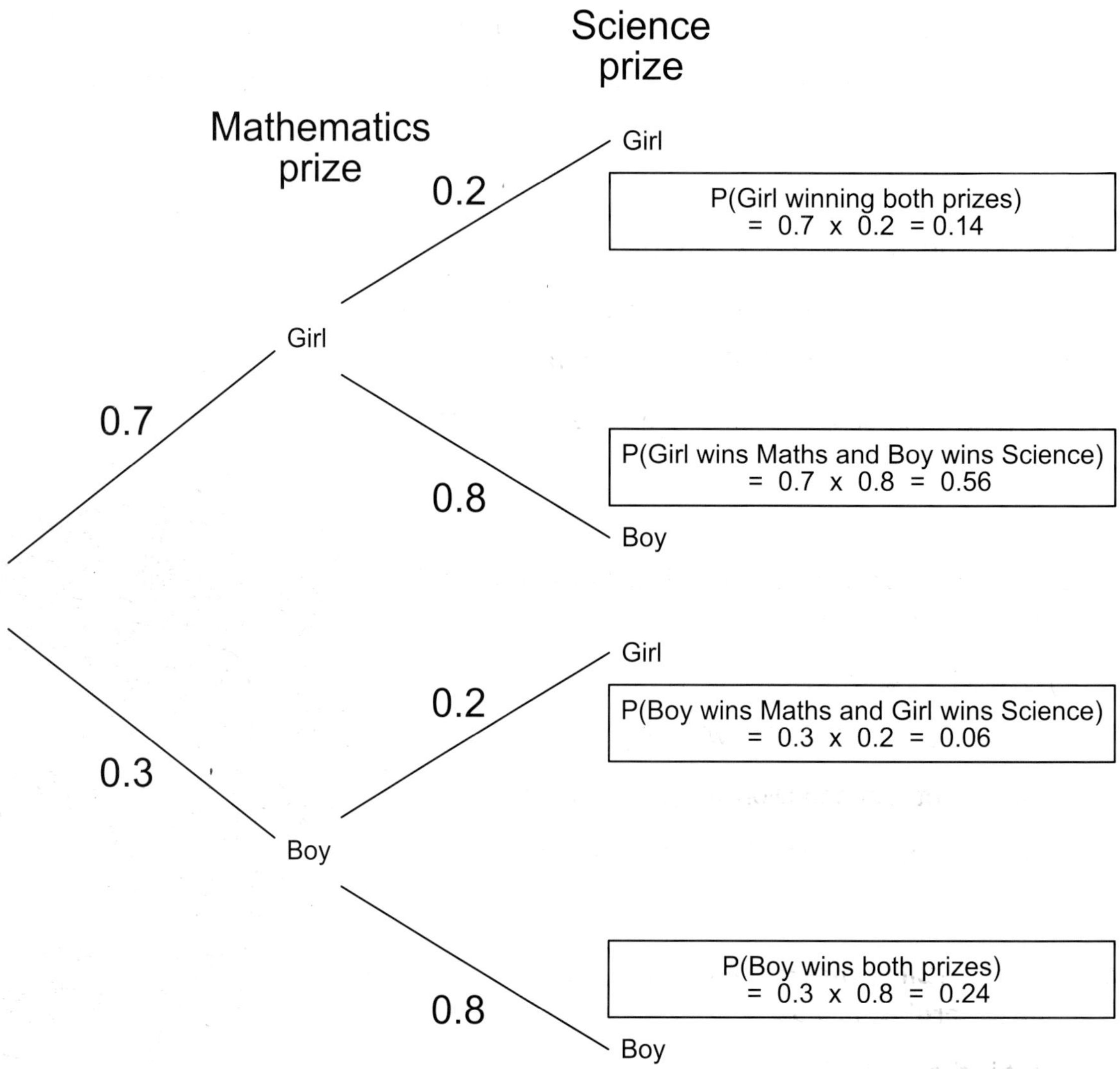

Notice the sum of all the probabilities is:

0.14 + 0.56 + 0.06 + 0.24 = 1

Probability 2 ~ Questions

1. Ahmed plays chess against Firas.

The probability that Ahmed wins is 0.4.

The probability that Firas wins is 0.3.

What is the probability of the result being a draw?

2. A competition involves a crisp manufacturer placing vouchers in packets of crisps.

The probability of a packet containing a voucher is $\frac{1}{10}$.

a) What is the probability that Sheila does not win a prize if she buys a packet of crisps?

b) What is the probability that she wins a prize if she buys two packets of crisps?

3. The probability that it will rain tomorrow is 0.6.

The probability that Dion will be going to school is 0.8.

a) What is the probability that it will not rain tomorrow

b) What is the probability that Dion does not go to school.

4. Draw a tree diagram and use it to help you find the following probabilities:

a) It will rain and Dion will go to school.

b) It will not rain and Dion will not go to school.

c) It will not rain and Dion will go to school.

d) It will rain and Dion will not go to school.

5. The probability that it will be freezing in the morning is 0.05.

What is the probability that it will not be freezing in the morning?

Euler's theorem

Here is a **cuboid**:

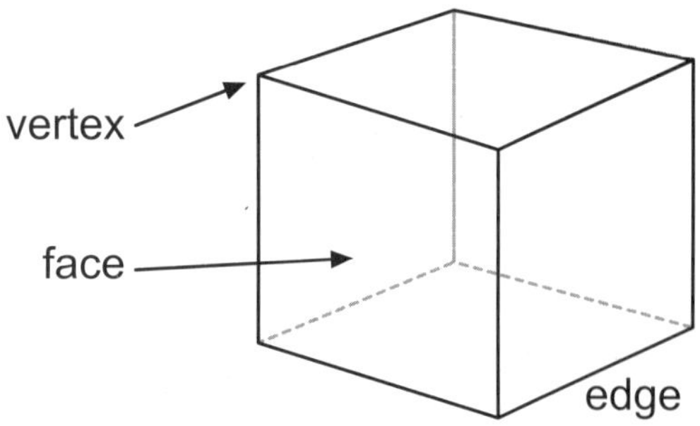

The cuboid has: 8 vertices, 6 faces and 12 edges.

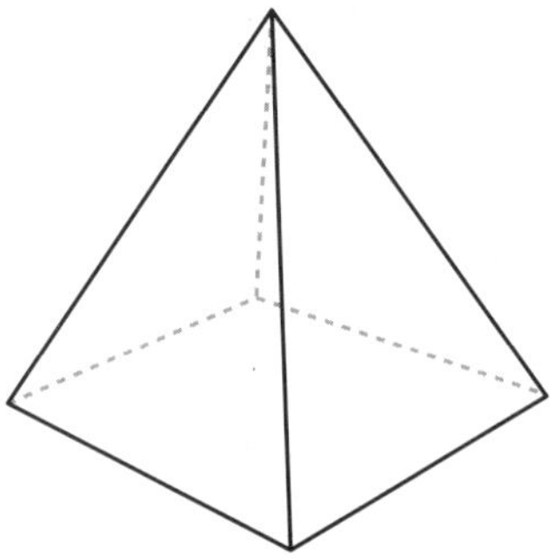

This is a square-based pyramid.

It has: 5 vertices, 5 faces and 8 edges.

1. Count the number of vertices, faces and edges on:

   a) a pentagonal-based prism

   b) a hexagonal-based pyramid

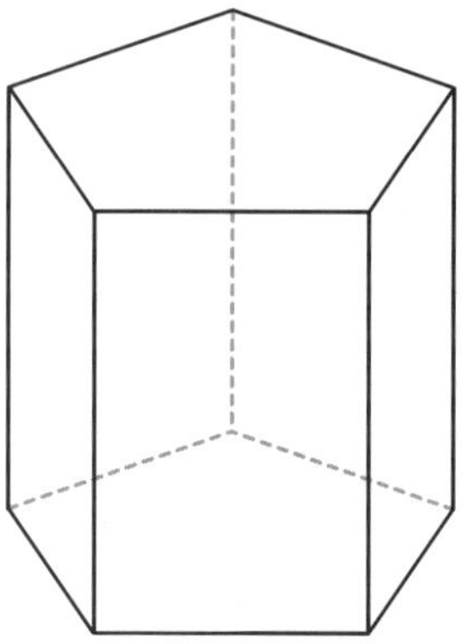

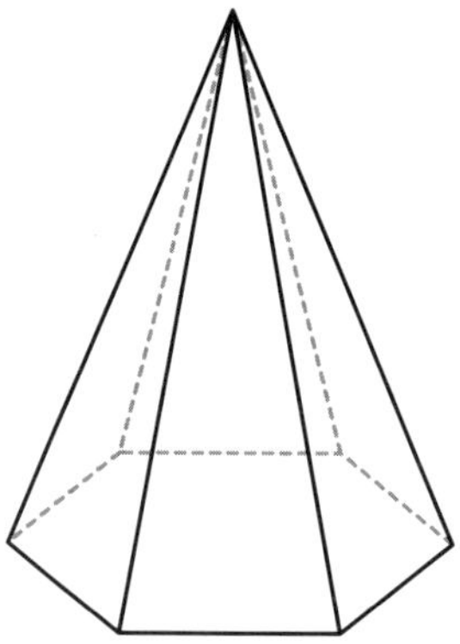

2. Copy and complete the table:

Shape	Vertices	Faces	Edges
Cuboid	8	6	12
Square pyramid	5	5	8
Pentagonal pyramid			
Hexagonal pyramid			

3. Try to find a **relationship** which **connects** the **numbers** of **vertices**, **faces** and **edges** for each of the above shapes.

Winners and losers

There are four horses in a race.

Their names are: **Amiable (A)** **Beauty (B)** **Cathy (C)** **Dynamite (D)**

One possible outcome of the race is that they finish in the order:

1st	2nd	3rd	4th
B	D	A	C

There can never be a dead heat.

1. List all the possible 24 outcomes of the race.

2. List all the possible outcomes of the race when Dynamite cannot run but the other three can.

3. How many different outcomes would there be in a race that has:

a) only two horses *(You can list these quite easily)*

b) five horses c) six horses d) seven horses *(Do not try to list these.)*

4. How many different outcomes would there be in a race that has n horses running in it?

Glossary

Angle: a measurement of turn.
Approximation: a rough answer which is usually made by rounding off numbers.
Area: the amount of space covered by a 2-D shape.
Average speed: the total distance travelled divided by the total time taken.

Bar chart: a diagram made up of a set of bars, of equal widths, and the lengths being proportional to a set of frequencies.
Bar line graph: a diagram made up of a set of straight lines with their heights or lengths being equal to a set of frequencies.
Bearing: an angle, measured in degrees from the North, in a clockwise direction.
Bias: an event which is more likely to give one outcome than any others.
Bisect: cut exactly in half.
Brackets: symbols which show those terms that should be dealt with together.

Capacity: the measure of the amount of space inside a 3-D object.
Circumference: the distance around the outside edge of a circle.
Class interval: a grouping of statistical data.
Coefficient: the number in front of a letter in an algebraic expression.
Complementary angles: two angles which add up to 90 degrees.
Congruent shapes: figures which are exactly the same size and shape.
Continuous data: data that is obtained by weighing or measuring.
Cumulative frequency: a running total of the frequencies.

Data: a collective name for pieces of information.
Degree: a unit for measuring an angle.
Denominator: the number on the bottom of a fraction.
Density: the mass per unit volume of a solid.
Diagonal: a line, which is not an edge, joining any two vertices of a shape.
Diameter: a straight line that passes through the centre of a circle.
Discrete data: data that can be counted.

Edge: where two faces meet in a 3-D shape.
Elevation: the view of a 3-D shape from its front, side, top or bottom.
Equation: a statement that two or more things are equal.
Evaluate: work out the value of an expression.
Expression: a collection of symbols which expresses a quantity.
Exterior angles: the angles on the outside of a polygon.

Face: one of the flat surfaces of a 3-D shape.
Factor: a number or expression that divides exactly into another number or expression.
Factorise: separate an expression into its factors.
Formula: a way of describing a rule using algebraic symbols.
Frequency: the number of times something has or should occur.
Frequency polygon: joins the midpoints of class intervals for grouped or continuous data.

Gradient: the slope of a line in relationship to the positive direction of the x-axis.
Greater than: something is bigger than something else.

Horizontal: a line going straight across.
Hypotenuse: the longest side of a right-angled triangle.
Hypothesis: a statement which can be tested to find out if it is true.

Independent events: two or more events which have no effect on each other.
Index: the power to which a quantity is raised.
Inequality: a statement that two or more things are not equal.
Integer: a positive or negative whole number.
Intercept: the point at which a graph crosses the vertical axis.
Interior angles: the angles on the inside of a polygon.
Isosceles triangle: a triangle with two equal angles and two equal sides.

Linear expression: one such as $3x + 2$ which, when drawn, gives a straight line.
Line graph: a graph formed by joining points with straight lines.
Locus: the set of all possible positions that a point can occupy, subject to various rules.
Lowest terms: for a fraction it means it cannot be cancelled down any further.

Mapping: a relationship between one set of numbers and another set of numbers.
Mean: the sum of all the values divided by the number of values.
Median: the middle value when a set of numbers is put in order of size.
Mode: the value that occurs most often.
Multiples: the numbers in the multiplication tables; e.g. 3, 6, 9, 12, are multiples of 3.
Multiplier: scale factor.
Mutually exclusive: events which cannot happen at the same time.

Net: a flat shape that can be folded into a 3-D solid.
Numerator: the top part of a fraction.

Outcome: possible results of a statistical experiment or an activity involving uncertainty.

Parallel lines: lines which are always the same distance apart.
Perimeter: distance around the outside edge of a shape.
Percentage: number of parts per a hundred.
Perpendicular: two lines which meet at ninety degrees.
Plan: the view of a 3-D shape when looked down on from above.
Polygon: a plane figure which has all of its sides as straight lines.
Prime number: a number which has only two factors.
Product: the result of two or more numbers being multiplied together.
Proportion: two quantities are in proportion if their ratio stays the same when the two quantities get smaller or larger.

Quadrilateral: a polygon with four sides.
Questionnaire: some sheets with questions which are used to collect data.
Radius: distance from the centre to a point on the circumference of the circle.
Range: the difference between the lowest and the highest number in a set of data.
Ratio: a way of showing the relationship or comparison between two numbers.
Reciprocal: one over a number.
Relative frequency: is used as an estimate of a probability.

Scale factor: the multiplier when a shape is enlarged or reduced in size.
Sequence: a set of numbers usually in a pattern.
Similar: two or more figures with the same shape but not the same size.
Standard form: a way of writing very large or small numbers in the form $a \times 10^n$ where n is an integer and $\leq a < 10$.
Substitution: replacing a letter with its numerical value.

Term: one of the parts of an expression.
Triangle: a polygon with three straight sides.

Variable: a quantity that can take a range of values.
Vector: a quantity that has both size and direction.
Vertical: a line that goes straight up and down.

x-axis: the horizontal axis.

y-axis: the vertical axis.

Index

Badger Publishing Limited
15 Wedgwood Gate, Pin Green Industrial Estate,
Stevenage, Hertfordshire SG1 4SU
Telephone: 01438 356907
Fax: 01438 747015
www.badger-publishing.co.uk
enquiries@badger-publishing.co.uk

SAT Attack
Badger Test Guides
Key Stage 3 Maths ~ Book 1
ISBN 1 84424 408 3

Publisher: David Jamieson
Editor: Paul Martin
Designer: Adam Wilmott
Illustrations: Adam Wilmott and Juliet Breese

Printed in the UK.